STEPPING STONES
— TO —
Recovery
From Codependency

Experience the miracle of 12 Step Recovery

Katie C. Deb M.

Cover design by
> Graphiti Associates, Inc.
> Seattle, Washington

Library of Congress Cataloging-in-Publication Data
Stepping stones to recovery from codependency : experience
the miracle of 12 step recovery / edited by Katie C. and Deb M.
— 1st ed.

      p.   cm.
      Includes index.
      ISBN 0-934125-24-4 : $7.95
      1.   Co-dependence (Psychology)—Miscellanea.
2. Twelve-step programs—Miscellanea. I. C., Katie.
II. M., Deb.
RC569.5.C63S74 1991
616.86—dc20   91-42366
                             CIP

First Edition

10 9 8 7 6 5 4 3 2 1

PREFACE

This collection of personal stories and topical articles is for all individuals in recovery from codependency. We are grateful to all of our fellow members in Co-Dependents Anonymous who have helped us through their interviews, comments, writings, and support during the preparation of this book, the first to bring together the shared experience of over 100 CoDA members.

We would like to thank Linda McClelland, Michelle Fujimoto, Kelly Pensell, and Todd Weber for their manuscript preparation and cover design. A special thank you to Bill Pittman, President of Glen Abbey Books, Inc., for believing in and guiding us through this project. Also to Scott M. for his patience and understanding, and Donna U. for her inspiration.

This book may be read straight through, or you can use the Daily Reading Guide to select one article to read each day.

We have both come to a deeper understanding of the beauty and restorative power of the program as a result of working on this book, and we hope you also will be benefited.

—Katie C.
—Deb M.

CONTENTS

DAILY READING GUIDE

January	February	March
1. p.11 #9	1. p.26 #21	1. p.41 #29
2. p.66 #50	2. p.75 #56	2. p.53 #38
3. p.29 #22	3. p.100 #73	3. p.129 #90
4. p.80 #59	4. p.147 #102	4. p.155 #107
5. p.107 #77	5. p.7 #6	5. p.98 #71
6. p.144 #100	6. p.87 #63	6. p.64 #48
7. p.69 #52	7. p.122 #84	7. p.104 #75
8. p.124 #86	8. p.177 #122	8. p.160 #110
9. p.159 #109	9. p.181 #125	9. p.171 #118
10. p.173 #120	10. p.48 #35	10. p.57 #42
11. p.49 #36	11. p.73 #54	11. p.77 #57
12. p.95 #68	12. p.128 #89	12. p.120 #83
13. p.178 #123	13. p.185 #127	13. p.186 #128
14. p.163 #112	14. p.55 #40	14. p.122 #84
15. p.86 #62	15. p.135 #94	15. p.25 #20
16. p.153 #106	16. p.74 #55	16. p.72 #53
17. p.174 #121	17. p.96 #69	17. p.136 #95
18. p.122 #85	18. p.187 #129	18. p.97 #70
19. p.6 #5	19. p.60 #44	19. p.182 #126
20. p.58 #43	20. p.134 #93	20. p.138 #96
21. p.109 #78	21. p.186 #128	21. p.21 #16
22. p.138 #96	22. p.168 #116	22. p.35 #25
23. p.165 #114	23. p.143 #99	23. p.125 #87
24. p.62 #46	24. p.52 #37	24. p.89 #64
25. p.90 #65	25. p.92 #66	25. p.43 #31
26. p.130 #91	26. p.152 #105	26. p.100 #73
27. p.171 #118	27. p.5 #4	27. p.19 #15
28. p.182 #126	28. p.89 #64	28. p.144 #100
29. p.114 #80	29. p.38 #27	29. p.116 #81
30. p.56 #41		30. p.95 #68
31. p.13 #11		31. p.1 #1

DAILY READING GUIDE

April	May	June
1. p.8 #7	1. p.48 #35	1. p.44 #32
2. p.54 #39	2. p.78 #58	2. p.90 #65
3. p.99 #72	3. p.124 #86	3. p.114 #80
4. p.172 #119	4. p.61 #45	4. p.53 #38
5. p.60 #44	5. p.142 #98	5. p.125 #87
6. p.100 #73	6. p.86 #62	6. p.171 #118
7. p.185 #127	7. p.145 #101	7. p.74 #55
8. p.149 #103	8. p.5 #4	8. p.134 #93
9. p.22 #17	9. p.58 #43	9. p.173 #120
10. p.118 #82	10. p.150 #104	10. p.7 #6
11. p.24 #19	11. p.23 #18	11. p.62 #46
12. p.64 #47	12. p.87 #63	12. p.104 #75
13. p.126 #88	13. p.106 #76	13. p.57 #42
14. p.161 #111	14. p.42 #30	14. p.96 #69
15. p.144 #100	15. p.159 #109	15. p.147 #102
16. p.31 #23	16. p.49 #36	16. p.52 #37
17. p.15 #12	17. p.56 #41	17. p.158 #108
18. p.136 #95	18. p.129 #90	18. p.66 #50
19. p.80 #59	19. p.164 #113	19. p.75 #56
20. p.12 #10	20. p.39 #28	20. p.138 #96
21. p.33 #24	21. p.94 #67	21. p.6 #5
22. p.84 #61	22. p.46 #34	22. p.97 #70
23. p.140 #97	23. p.18 #14	23. p.25 #20
24. p.45 #33	24. p.155 #107	24. p.165 #114
25. p.111 #79	25. p.174 #121	25. p.35 #25
26. p.3 #3	26. p.29 #22	26. p.116 #81
27. p.69 #52	27. p.179 #124	27. p.153 #106
28. p.130 #91	28. p.3 #2	28. p.73 #54
29. p.11 #9	29. p.9 #8	29. p.122 #84
30. p.16 #13	30. p.55 #40	30. p.13 #11
	31. p.37 #26	

DAILY READING GUIDE

July	August	September
1. p.3 #3	1. p.9 #8	1. p.35 #25
2. p.54 #39	2. p.64 #48	2. p.89 #64
3. p.111 #79	3. p.118 #82	3. p.134 #93
4. p.149 #103	4. p.143 #99	4. p.60 #44
5. p.21 #16	5. p.80 #59	5. p.94 #67
6. p.87 #63	6. p.23 #18	6. p.142 #98
7. p.144 #100	7. p.107 #77	7. p.99 #72
8. p.41 #29	8. p.164 #113	8. p.13 #11
9. p.161 #111	9. p.61 #45	9. p.49 #36
10. p.42 #30	10. p.136 #95	10. p.100 #73
11. p.140 #97	11. p.159 #109	11. p.150 #104
12. p.68 #51	12. p.26 #21	12. p.66 #50
13. p.152 #105	13. p.82 #60	13. p.90 #65
14. p.15 #12	14. p.31 #23	14. p.5 #4
15. p.65 #49	15. p.120 #83	15. p.53 #38
16. p.170 #117	16. p.48 #35	16. p.101 #74
17. p.22 #17	17. p.92 #66	17. p.44 #32
18. p.33 #24	18. p.126 #88	18. p.122 #85
19. p.39 #28	19. p.64 #47	19. p.158 #108
20. p.109 #78	20. p.106 #76	20. p.62 #46
21. p.24 #19	21. p.55 #40	21. p.129 #90
22. p.163 #112	22. p.12 #10	22. p.46 #34
23. p.38 #27	23. p.3 #2	23. p.138 #96
24. p.128 #89	24. p.16 #13	24. p.29 #22
25. p.1 #1	25. p.18 #14	25. p.122 #84
26. p.72 #53	26. p.58 #43	26. p.165 #114
27. p.172 #119	27. p.95 #68	27. p.69 #52
28. p.167 #115	28. p.11 #9	28. p.130 #91
29. p.45 #33	29. p.56 #41	29. p.43 #31
30. p.19 #15	30. p.84 #61	30. p.7 #6
31. p.8 #7	31. p.37 #26	

DAILY READING GUIDE

1. WHAT IS CODEPENDENCE?

These patterns and characteristics are offered as a tool to aid in self-evaluation. They may be particularly helpful to newcomers as they begin to understand codependence and may aid those who have been in recovery awhile in determining what traits still need attention and transformation.

Denial Patterns:

I have difficulty identifying what I am feeling.

I minimize, alter, or deny how I truly feel.

I perceive myself as completely unselfish and dedicated to the well-being of others.

Low Self-esteem Patterns:

I have difficulty making decisions.

I judge everything I think, say, or do harshly, as never "good enough."

I am embarrassed to receive recognition and praise or gifts.

I do not ask others to meet my needs or desires.

I value others' approval of my thinking, feelings, and behaviors over my own.

I do not perceive myself as a lovable or worthwhile person.

Compliance Patterns:

I compromise my own values and integrity to avoid rejection or others' anger.

I am very sensitive to how others are feeling and feel the *same*.

I am extremely loyal, remaining in harmful situations too long.

I value others' opinions and feelings more than my own and am often afraid to express differing opinions and feelings of my own.

I put aside my own interests and hobbies in order to do what others want.

I accept sex when I want love.

Control Patterns:

I believe most other people are incapable of taking care of themselves.

I attempt to convince others of what they "should" think and how they "truly" feel.

I become resentful when others will not let me help them.

I freely offer others advice and directions without being asked.

I lavish gifts and favors on those I care about.

I use sex to gain approval and acceptance.

I have to be "needed" in order to have a relationship with others.

2. MY BILL OF RIGHTS

I have the right to:
be treated with respect.
say no and not feel guilty.
experience and express my feelings.
take time for myself.
change my mind.
ask for what I want.
ask for information.
make mistakes.
do less than I am humanly capable of.
feel good about myself.
act only in ways that promote my dignity and self-respect as long as others' are not violated in the process.

3. WE

The first word of the First Step is WE. So my sponsor and I (we) did it together. We met at a coffee shop. Per her direction, I brought my dictionary, my Big Book, paper, pencil, an open mind, and an attitude of gratitude.

We broke the Step into sections: We; Admitted; That we were powerless; Over other people; That our lives had become; Unmanageable. These Steps were written by people who were willing to do anything to save their lives. "Are you?" she asked. I answered "Yes," but I really wasn't sure what I was in for. WE found out.

Together, we looked up each of the six sections in the dictionary, and checked definitions of definitions for clarity. We found workable definitions, ones that I could grab hold of, because my life depended on working and living with the tools of the Steps. We began to build a foundation for me to find a new way to live.

I asked if this was how *her* sponsor had helped her to know WE. She said yes. She had such a look of love about her, but somehow she knew where my mind was headed. She smiled and asked, "Could you learn how to swim by reading a book?" Well, technically, but it wouldn't be the same.... I knew what she was getting at. "It would seem to be easy for me to give you the work that I have done, that my sponsor did, that her sponsor did, but that would cheat you out of the experience. We will get in the water together and we will stay in the water while you practice."

I don't know yet why I want to talk my way around or through things, but I do. I feel compelled to at least give it my best shot. Every ounce of me wants to argue that I am different, that I can swim without the water, and I definitely can swim without WE. I felt waves of anger and fear run through me as we discussed this. She knows, she nods her head a lot. "But, but, but," I sputter. "Are you willing to go to any lengths to get different?" she asks. I sit back and breathe. "Yes, I am willing..." "Good, that is all that is required right now."

4. ADMITTED

My sponsor told me that she didn't totally understand "how" the Steps worked, but she did understand that the original writers, the AAs, said "precisely" when they described how the Big Book gave direction. So we follow in their footsteps, precisely.

We looked up "admitted" in the dictionary. She pointed out that someone had to do the admitting. I immediately said, "WE!" I was encouraged. I wasn't alone. We were working together. I had always thought of admitting as giving information over to another person, but after looking it up, I found that it meant *to own, accept, acknowledge* and that "accept" meant *to confess, or agree with*. My definition became a picture in my head of a little child receiving a gift. And then we expanded the picture to be a room of little children each receiving a gift.

5.   POWERLESS

My sponsor cautioned me that these words (as all words in any one Step) did not stand alone. We were seizing their essence, but would use them in conjunction with the whole.

Without the ability to produce or act, was what my dictionary offered for "powerless." For me to experience this, I had to make two lists for us to go over. The first was a list of the people, places, and things that I was grateful for. We called this my "joy list." It started with me, then expanded. I was told to be specific, that each list was a brick in the foundation of my recovery.

Starting the list, I felt a little annoyed and anxious to get it done so I could share about having worked my First Step at a meeting. "These are a few of my favorite things" drifted through my head, lightening my spirit, and I began: snowflakes, lightning in August, falling stars, my nose so I can smell the orange blossoms, the taste of good turkey gravy and the smell of turkey in the oven, the sound of wind in the pine trees, all that I love. I felt like the luckiest person in the whole world. Thoughts flew through my head, and I wrote until they stopped. I couldn't wait to share with my sponsor. Before we talked about it though, she made me make the second list.

6. UNMANAGEABLE

This list consisted of those things that no matter how hard I tried, frustrated me, or really made me mad. These were the things that I couldn't manage to control. As I wrote down each one I felt madder and madder. Finally, I got so irritated I couldn't write anymore. I gave the list to my sponsor and told her that I didn't appreciate being manipulated like a puppet. I fumed. I was surprised that she seemed to agree with my anger. It encouraged me and I really told her what I thought. "And how do you feel?" she asked. I gave her an earful there, too.

"Good," she said. "You are growing and beginning to live the First Step." I found no comfort in her words, but she caught my attention. "Step one is like breathing," she added. "We depend on it for life. God gives us the power to do it. We can alter our pattern, but we cannot hold our breath indefinitely." I thought she made sense even though I was not a Christian or a church-goer.

After just sitting together quietly for a few seconds, she asked me to get out both my gratitude list and my unmanageable list. We talked about the common ingredient of both the seemingly good and seemingly bad: powerlessness. When I liked it, it seemed good and I felt joy. When I didn't like it, it seemed

bad and I felt frustrated or angry. She pointed out
that in either case, I had no control over the situation.
I felt terribly ashamed as she talked. I felt like a bad
person, as if I had done something wrong. I felt as if
I wasn't enough. We talked about my feelings. She
reminded me that it was not a good or bad issue. She
told me that she had confused good, bad, and powerless until she began to practice Step One.

She also told me that as we worked through all of
the Steps that I would gain an understanding of how
creative I had been at denying the fear of being powerless. Admitting it begins our solution.

7.   OSTRICH

Now that I'm in recovery I don't have to hide
from situations that used to scare me. This doesn't
mean that I go out to the busiest street and stand in
front of trucks. I still have common sense. In fact, I
am even more able to use it and apply it to those fright-
ening times when I feel threatened.

My old way of doing things was to hide, or do it
your way. Now I use the new way of thinking I have
learned in recovery. Sayings like "I am a worthy
child of God and my ideas count" help me a lot.

Before, I used to feel as if bombs were hitting me
and that my only option was to run and hide, like an

ostrich. Now I know that usually things don't happen all at once. The Fourth Step has helped me see patterns building up. I have learned that by loving myself and praying to my Higher Power for courage, I can speak my mind lovingly and gently (or even forcefully, if needed) and not cheat myself out of life.

This new respect I have learned to give myself has freed me to respect others more, too. Listening to myself, thinking, and respecting my own feelings are tools for building healthy boundaries.

Yes, I still get frightened, but the more I practice this new way of life, the more comfortable I get. It is so wonderful not to have my head buried in the sand all the time! I am able to face life on life's terms now that I have the tools of recovery.

8. DECISIONS

Making a decision, whether it be a small one to take an umbrella with us in the morning, or a big one to change jobs, is a part of life that many of us have trouble with.

There are myriad factors that enter into decision-making. For self-confident people it may be a breeze. For those of us who live with the problems of codependency, whose self-confidence and self-esteem have been eroded by the confusion in our lives, decision-making can be fraught with peril. The old *what-ifs* come flooding into our minds. The thought of spouse or family's not approving our decision can paralyze us.

One saving thought, to me, was that most times the decision was not earthshaking, that there was not a 100% right answer, simply a choice. Painting the kitchen white or pale yellow, for instance. The kitchen was going to look great either color because it would sparkle with fresh clean paint.

It also helped me to tell myself not to sweat the small decisions. Doing that, I realized, wasted my energy and affected my ability to concentrate.

"Take your time!" was another helpful phrase. I needed time to reflect on the important decisions. Feeling rushed is the way to impulsive decisions we may be unhappy with. "Sleep on it" is a very good saying that pays off. The bright light of morning may find us more clear-headed and hopeful.

There is help. I found that friends in the Program who listened and then shared their experience with me were able to give me a new perspective. They also boosted my morale and that made decision-making easier. When several people say, "You can do it," you find yourself saying, "Hey! Maybe I can!"

Ours is a spiritual Program. We learn that turning to our Higher Power and listening for His guidance can lead to resolutions we may never have thought of otherwise. Looking back, I realize that my thinking had become rigid and fearful. Asking for His help opened windows in my mind and allowed a fresh clean breeze to sweep through. I could then apply myself to reviewing my options and considering the consequences of different possibilities.

I think the saying, "progress, not perfection," helped me, too. Not requiring perfection of myself left me free to choose the best possibility, to change my mind when that seemed right and to be open to nonconventional thinking. Feeling free is a tremendous start in decision-making. I had to learn not to become obsessed with decisions.

Using the wisdom of the Program, I built my confidence very gradually until I was able to consider problems without panic, but with trust in myself and faith in my Higher Power.

9. EXPECTATIONS

Examining my life in Step Four and talking to my sponsor in Step Five gave me a way to apply the first three Steps. I knew I was powerless over others, but I didn't know how to stop that dance I did that seemed always to lead to my doing it someone else's way and neglecting my own needs.

I discovered that I invited others into the codependent relationships because I expected them to be different than they really were. Yes, I discovered others' defects were obvious, but now that I knew I couldn't change them, I could change me. Instead of telling my mom about school (she always responded negatively), I learned to tell someone who supported me. Instead of expecting my dad to hug me and father me (he never had those skills), I learned to get my hugs at meetings from my new family.

I needed to be supported and loved. I just kept expecting people to meet those needs who didn't and never had.

Letting go of expectations has been part of my Step work. It has given my parents the freedom to be who they are and allowed me the freedom to accept them for who they are instead of trying to make them into what they "should" be. I get the validation I need and I can see my parents for themselves.

10. DETACHMENT

I like to think of detachment as one of our best tools against the effects of codependency in our lives. It must be used carefully and not confused with "indifference." I can tell whether I am detaching or being indifferent, simply by my attitude. I can't remember feeling more *alone* than when I practiced indifference.

Detachment is a lovely thing. It allows me to walk through life peacefully, without all those fears and frustrations weighing me down. Although I wasn't aware of it at the time, detachment was a very important first step toward learning to see myself clearly as an individual.

Since I have unglued myself from other people's problems and choices, I can concentrate on my own life and responsibilities, my own growth and spirituality.

11. LIVING IN TODAY

I had five years of recovery from addiction to alcohol and pills. I was in therapy. After a two-year absence from Twelve Step meetings, I had joined a home group and gotten a sponsor. I was desperate for recovery and not just freedom from "picking up the next one."

In therapy I had remembered that as a child, I had been sexually abused. My mind made jumps from that event to my continued sexual victimization to addiction to the present. No wonder I was so miserable. I raced to my home group and cornered my sponsor before the meeting. She was a tough old gal, a real honest, down-to-earth Arizona woman. As I poured out my revelations, she spat back, "You aren't a victim. You're a volunteer."

I paled and stiffened and started to "But..." and she asked me what I was doing today about the solution. "Look," she said. "Yes, your trust, your very sense of self was violated repeatedly. You grew up; it was lousy. So what are you going to do about it?"

When I couldn't answer, she continued, "I think you're mentally repeating those violations over and over. That doesn't get you out of the problem and into the solution. It gives you an excuse to keep living in the blame. You were a victim, hah! You keep at it. Meet me for coffee after the meeting."

Not surprisingly, the chairperson chose "Just For Today" as the topic. I heard others share how they found freedom from the pain of the past by accepting the hope of Step Two to have a Higher Power restore them to sanity. My sponsor's words rang in my head. Then I heard someone share about the courage given with Step Three to live in today.

I realized that I could feel the feelings of my past without getting stuck in them. I could live happy, joyous, and free today, by living in the solution. It was this solution that could give me the freedom to use the past as an asset, instead of staying a victim full of blame.

Living in today I don't have to control what happened to me yesterday. I don't have to figure everything out by playing "what ifs" and "if onlies." Living in today I have come to believe that God will restore me to sanity. I will let Him.

At coffee after the meeting I told my sponsor about my realizations. We talked about how we could apply the Steps. We had coffee today, laughed about today, shared about today. We lived Today.

12. THE VIEW FROM THE TOP

When I first entered the Program, being the impatient person that I am, I wasted a lot of time looking for the elevator. I wanted to find a fast, easy way to the top, to serenity.

As you know, there isn't one. Instead, I found Twelve (sometimes very steep) Steps. I have come to realize there is a reason for each one.

Suppose you were going to climb a tall tower and you were given a choice between a dizzyingly fast ride to the top in an elevator in which all you had to look at during the trip were four uninteresting walls, and a winding staircase with a beautiful view of the landscape from windows on each landing.

The Steps provide us with the same opportunity, the chance to see ourselves, our situations, those around us and, ultimately, our Higher Power, in another perspective.

In the First Step, we are given a view of the codependent situation as something over which we are powerless. Step Four allows us to get a good look at ourselves through a personal inventory and in Step Five we are able to experience the loving acceptance of another member by sharing our wrongs with him or her. As we reach Step Eleven and establish a conscious contact with our Higher Power, the view becomes glorious indeed, and well worth the climb.

Literature, the slogans and Twelve Traditions are like refreshments along the way up. Imagine, however, how difficult it would be to climb those steep Steps without a handrail. In CoDA, the members are that handrail, offering a sturdy support for those who are willing to reach out and grab hold.

I'm ever grateful for the Steps, the handrail, and for the view from the top.

13. LADY

Like most females, I was taught in my childhood to be a "good girl." To my folks, that meant being smart in school, keeping myself and my room clean, helping my grandmother in the kitchen, deferring to my brothers and my dad "because they're the boys," never talking back to grownups—in general, being a "lady," instead of the tomboy I really was.

"Ladies don't get their dresses dirty." "Ladies don't say those words" (this after I tried out a few I'd heard my brothers use). "Ladies serve the family first." "Ladies take care of the house and kids; gentlemen work and bring home money, which ladies ask for to run the house."

It was quite a shock to me when I realized how many of those "lady" statements were still running my life thirty years later. The message was, it was wrong for me to ask for help around the house—I "should" be able to take care of everything myself. If I was tired and cranky, too bad—the family came before my feelings, and I "should" hide my exhaustion and be cheerful for them. My children had to be the best at everything, because they were my identity as a "lady." No wonder I was full of resentments, anger, and hurt!

It's such a relief not to have to be perfect any more. Admitting I couldn't cope with everything felt like the end of the world. Now I am amazed how much lighter I feel. It's still a constant struggle to turn loose of control, but now I'm happy being a fallible, human, imperfect *woman* instead of a "lady."

14. FIXING OTHERS

One of the first things we hear when we start recovery is "don't fix; be supportive." If it was within our capacity to fix people's lives, we would have done so a long time ago with all our friends and relatives. We finally realized in our First Step how hopelessly mismatched we were for the job of fixing ourselves and the whole world. Most of us struggled for years to fix our own lives, but we couldn't. It wasn't until we admitted we were licked that we finally got the help we needed. By working the other eleven Steps, we came to believe that a Power greater than ourselves could fix what we couldn't.

Our roles in life change as a result of the Steps. We watch the way God might be moving in the life of a friend or loved one, and we try to support God's handiwork. We watch the ways our fellow members offer support, always encouraging us to accept situations we can't change, or to get back to change situations we can.

When we try to fix others, it doesn't work very well. All we can really do is be supportive in their efforts and focus on fixing ourselves.

15. BROKEN RECORD

Steps 6 and 7 provided me with my first chance to walk through the quicksand of issues. I had my list of character defects. I had my list of assets. I had a sense of willingness to get rid of all those rocks in my garden of life. I felt that I humbly wanted to be rid of them. The problem was I hadn't really accepted the truth of who I was in Step 5.

I didn't find this out right away. It came only after weeks of struggling with feelings of dissatisfaction and disillusionment. In spite of reading all the materials on the Steps, talking to my sponsor, sharing at meetings, I felt like a broken record.

By going back over my daily journal, and soliciting some honest feedback, I realized I had looked at my character defects as if they were a coat I had worn for a long time. I felt I should just be able to take it off and be done with it. I hated that coat. I didn't want to be associated with it. I was embarrassed by it.

Diseased thinking was controlling my life once again. I got stuck in the good/bad syndrome. I got addicted to my issues. I knew we didn't get sick overnight and I wasn't going to get well overnight, and I sure got a lot of mileage out of that idea. I had a pair of issue-colored glasses and everywhere I looked, everything I read or did was issue-oriented. Like the quicksand, the more I wriggled around, the deeper I got into the problem, the more stuck I got—a broken record.

I was so dumbstruck by what I learned about myself in Step Five that I kept repeating it: the happy childhood that wasn't, the attentive mom who wasn't, the damaged child. Over and over I talked about how bad it was, how it colored my very life, and how I was working on my issues by working Steps and getting professional help. All this was true; I had been damaged, abused, ignored, victimized, and I needed to talk about it. I needed help in getting different.

I just didn't know I was stuck in the process, nor did I know that I didn't have to stay stuck. I looked around me and saw that others in recovery also had these experiences. They were laughing and living. Why wasn't I? I was continuing to color my life with yesterday.

I went back to Step Five. This time I was able to allow myself to feel the feelings. I was afraid it would be a bottomless pit of rage and sadness. It wasn't. It was sad, and I was angry, but I could feel those feelings for yesterday and not get stuck. I could have freedom today.

I don't know if I will ever reach the last day that I mourn my childhood, but today, I live in today. I celebrate that no one is beating me today. The best part is that I now have the tools of Steps 6 and 7 to walk around the quicksand. I have responsibility for me and I am grateful and free from the broken record of my old life.

16. WHERE DO WE GO FROM HERE?

Sometimes, even after we identify a Taker in our lives, we wind up compromising between their demands and our needs. Takers often challenge the boundaries we try to set with them, or dishonor those boundaries altogether. Takers can wear us down. They may attempt to manipulate situations, because that was the prior pattern of our dealings with them. When we let them do this, we make ourselves into victims again.

In recovery, we are told to accept with unconditional love. That doesn't mean we should allow a Taker's destructive behavior to hurt us. Unconditional love means loving ourselves enough to say no, and keep on saying it as long as necessary to get our point across. Recovery gives us the strength and hope to accomplish this.

17. ROAD TO TRUSTING

I have been a member of CoDA for two years. The journey has been eventful, the road uneven, but I have not travelled alone.

I enjoyed the support, confidence, and love of my group at first, combined later with trust and guidance in a Higher Power of my choice.

I was so sick with resentment and self-pity I was slow to learn how to detach and not judge. I divorced the alcoholic in my life and found life still unmanageable. I could not divorce my children. I have learned to let them go, one at a time, and the rewards have been tremendous. As a result I experienced relationships with honesty, dignity, tolerance, and love—a first for me. CoDA gave me the tools: my meetings, the slogans, Steps, and Traditions.

The relationship I am working on today is with myself. Participation in the Program gives me confidence and courage. I am beginning to know myself and continually focus on Steps Three and Eleven. I still operate with resistance, which I find almost as tiring as resentment. I found Step Seven and it helps.

I have trust in my Higher Power and try to be tolerant toward myself, keep enthusiastic, and go slow. To get in tune with that Power I turned to nature. Once in touch with the natural rhythm and beauty of life I am able, once again, to focus on what I can do instead of what I cannot. I know there is a solution for every problem, a way through.

Today I have made progress with gentleness, courage, gratitude, hope, and forgiveness.

18. MY MOTHER HAD EYES IN THE BACK OF HER HEAD

My sisters and I modified the song about "Santa Claus Is Coming To Town." "Mom knows when you've been sleeping, she knows when you're awake, she knows when you've been bad or good, so be good or die." No, she wouldn't have hit us, much less kill us, but those looks! We were afraid to even breathe crooked. It was the way I grew up. It was the way I thought life was supposed to be.

I learned right from wrong on my mother's yard-stick, not mine. I learned how to meet her needs, soothe her moods, and carry her shame. I was good at it. The better I got, the further I got from me, and the more codependent I became. Since my sense of wrong ("should not") came from the outside, I became accustomed to denying my own inner voice. It was a way to avoid confusion. By pleasing others I didn't have to choose between me or them; I just ignored me. This also meant that my sense of right ("should") had to come from the outside. My sense of self, of who I was, what I wanted from life, was whatever someone else said I should do.

This codependent thinking required me to have "other-esteem," not self-esteem. My whole lifestyle attracted people with eyes in the backs of their heads. It was a lock-and-key fit, and it was a trap that had no end unless I learned to do it differently.

I had always thought that if only others weren't the way they were, I could be different. When I found recovery, I learned it was me who had to change. It wasn't about whether Santa Claus, my mom, or anyone else had eyes in the backs of their heads. It was about me rediscovering the voice inside that I had so skillfully learned to dismiss, deny, and avoid.

19. CRISIS LIVING

Before I started recovery, I was one of those people who live from crisis to crisis. If there didn't happen to be one, I would create one. My greatest fear was that life would be "boring."

I did this by controlling situations and people through lack of control. I put off making decisions until they were made for me by others, with the result that I spent a lot of my time being told what to do by someone else—bill collectors, my children, my husband, my friends. This gave me someone to blame when things didn't go the way I wanted them to go. It wasn't my fault. I was too busy "coping with everything" to take care of the detail work. It was someone else's job, not mine, to regulate my life. I was too involved with living from one catastrophe to another to see the next one coming.

Now, when I find myself sliding back into this way of thinking, I stop and take a deep breath. I think about what the consequences will be if I don't make a decision at this moment. Will waiting create a crisis? If it will, then even a small decision is better than none.

With the help of my Higher Power, my sponsor, and my fellow members, I'm working toward meeting challenges, not making crises. Far from being boring, my life is new, exciting, and happy.

20. COMMUNICATION

The most difficult part of communication for me is actually getting the words out of my mouth. I often still have difficulty getting that first word out, but once I express myself, it's great! No guilt, no more resentments.

Sometimes there is a great deal of anxiety associated with communicating a boundary to someone I feel has violated it. I learned not to spend too much time planning word-for-word what I was going to say. I concentrate on being honest, and express myself with "I" statements, avoiding the word "you."

For example, I might tell my daughter, "I feel uncomfortable when you rummage through my hand-bag. I keep everything in an order that suits me. I would be willing to help you find something that has been misplaced, but I want to go through my own handbag." The example uses "I feel...." The second sentence gives a reason why I feel that way. The third statement offers a compromise that I am comfortable with, and solves any anxiety my daughter may have about being confronted.

To sum up: I try to be clear, give my reasons, and offer a solution with which I am comfortable. Effective communication requires courage, but it's well worth the effort, and gets easier each time.

21. BUT I'M NOT AN ADDICT—AM I?

I knew that I was a Supermom type. It seemed to give me such pleasure to have all the bases covered. I had no children of my own, but I considered the neighborhood my family, and therefore my responsibility. I needed to be busy, and not only didn't mind, but depended on my "family" to keep me busy. I ran errands, taxied kids to school, old Mrs. Ollan to the doctor, lent money, and bought special little gifts for everyone. I kept doggie and kitty treats in my pockets and a full water dish out for birds. I was prepared.

Although I hated housework, I made sure my house was comfortably clean in case someone dropped in. I kept the snacks and beverages I thought were favorites of my friends so they would know they were welcome. I just didn't feel right if I failed to anticipate the needs of my family.

It was true that many on the block thought I was a little strange. I didn't mind, though. Being the eccentric old maid was O.K. At least they knew they could call on me day or night for anything and they wouldn't get turned down. I was never too busy to be "there" for them. It was my life.

Almost everything was wonderful, but I had serious blue days. I didn't know it was depression. I would just need to take a few days every couple of weeks to reorient, charge my batteries, and get caught up so I could be strong again.

A neighbor's husband went into a Twelve Step treatment center program and she went to the group for spouses. Of course I supported her. She was too afraid to be alone, and I went to her meetings with her. At the meetings they talked about addictive behavior. Of course she had it, she was married to an alcoholic.

But I felt so uncomfortable about the descriptions they were using.

They said addictive behavior was not about the substance, it was about repeating behavior and ignoring the negative consequences. The example that hit me hardest was neglecting our own needs in order to forever accommodate the needs of others, repeating this until exhausted and then suffering through a time of depression because our own needs were not being fulfilled. They talked about the difference of helping others by being of service to them and helping others to be of service to ourselves because of codependency.

I recognized the term from the talk shows, but never, until then, had I thought it applied to me. Their description of addictive behavior *was* about me, though, and it scared me. I wanted to stop living. I feared that I was codependent. It was true what they said, I didn't feel good about me unless you felt good about you. I couldn't take time to go to the dentist, but I could make sure you went. They said that these were symptoms of people who felt they didn't deserve life, that only others did, so they devoted their lives to others. That was me. I was addicted to others. They also said that this group was designed to help, and then they asked if there were any who would like to join. By then, I had forgotten that I had come to support my friend. I raised my hand. I wanted what they had. I never knew it could be different, that I could have life, too. Now, I wanted it. That's how I joined CODA.

22. BEING WHO I AM

Sister, friend, worker, student, helper, volunteer—but who am I really? Learning to be true to myself entailed finding out who I was. Step Four led me to inventory my thoughts, behavior patterns, and responses. I feared I would come up with an empty shell who did not have life except as a reflection of the world around me. I feared I was so unlikable that I had created the codependent me, and that person was the only one (always pleasing you) that would be acceptable. I was terrified, yet hopeful that the process would lead me to the freedom I saw in others.

I found that my list of defects and my list of assets were similar. I learned that I needed to treat myself the way I would treat my best friend. All the caring, nurturing, and helping skills I had always applied to everyone else were what I needed to do for me. I was a "make-better" kind of person; I just didn't have any balance. I had been there for others for so long I had forgotten who I was. When I nurtured myself, I nurtured only those aspects which I believed you liked, and when I did that I not only lied to you and cheated you out of knowing me as a real human being, I cheated me. I kept me from being me, and as I did that, the real me cried out, acted out, and came out sideways resentful and victimized.

Through a life of codependency I had learned roles to keep me busy and give me my identity. These roles seemed easy at the time. I could be perfect at them, but I was never me and never happy. The roles had easily definable walls, but these walls kept me from the love and intimacy I was starved for. They kept out the things I was afraid of, but they also kept out the things I needed.

I learned that by cherishing myself, I could learn what I wanted, liked, and didn't like. Using the Steps as tools and sharing at meetings gave me an opportunity to set boundaries that protected me, taught me to respect the boundaries of others, and showed me how to live a real life. I felt like a little kid in a candy store. I had so much to try. What did I like? What did I want? Being me was not about being good or bad, it was about being real and learning to live life on life's terms. It was so free to be able to make decisions for me. At first I experienced a lot of fear and guilt, but I found that the more I was me, the more I could let you be you, and the more we liked each other.

I don't like everyone and of course not everyone likes me, but the best part is that I like me. I am amazed that many of the characteristics I've admired in others really exist in me. I have the freedom of choice to grow and change and make mistakes and not be perfect. I have the freedom to be me.

23. DROP THE ROCK

Seems there was this group of 12 Step members taking a boat ride to this island called SERENITY, and they were truly a happy bunch of people. As the boat pulled away from the dock, a few on board noticed Mary running down the street trying to catch up with the boat. One said, "Darn, she's missed the boat." Another said, "Maybe not. Come on, Mary! Jump in the water! Swim! Swim! You can make it! You can catch up with us!"

So Mary jumped into the water and started to swim for all she was worth. She swam for quite a while, and then started to sink. The members on board, now all aware that Mary was struggling, shouted, "Come on, Mary! Don't give up! Drop the rock!" With that encouragement, Mary started swimming again, only to start sinking again shortly afterward. She was going under when she heard all those voices shouting to her, "Mary, drop the rock! Let go, and drop the rock!"

Mary was vaguely aware of something around her neck, but she couldn't quite figure out what it was. Once more, she gathered her strength and started swimming. She was doing quite well, even gaining a little on the boat, but then she felt this heaviness pulling her under again. She saw all those people on the boat holding out their hands and hollering for her to keep swimming and shouting, "Don't be an idiot, Mary! Drop the rock!"

Then she understood, when she was going down for the third time. This thing around her neck, *this* was why she kept sinking when she really *wanted* to catch the boat. This thing was the "rock" they were all shouting about: resentments, fear, dishonesty, self-pity, intolerance and anger, just some of the things her "rock" was made of. "Get rid of the rock," she told herself. "Now! Get rid of it!"

So Mary managed to stay afloat long enough to untangle a few of the strings holding that rock around her neck, realizing as she did that her load was easing up; and then, with another burst of energy, she Let Go. She tore the other strings off and Dropped the Rock.

Once free of the rock, she was amazed how easy it was to swim, and she soon caught up with the boat. Those on board were cheering for her and applauding and telling her how great she was, and how it was so good having her with them again, and how now we can get on with our boat ride and have a nice time.

Mary felt great and was just about to indulge in a little rest and relaxation when she glanced back to shore. There, a ways back, she thought she saw something bobbing in the water, so she pointed it out to some others. Sure enough, someone was trying to catch the boat, swimming for dear life but not making much headway. In fact, it looked like they were going under.

Mary looked around and saw the concern on the faces of the other members. She was the first to lean over the rail and shout, "Hey, friend! Drop the Rock!"

24. BALANCE

As codependents, we spend our lifetimes giving or taking too much, particularly from those we love and care for the most. Breaking the old routine and learning a new balance of give and take is difficult, not only for us, but also for the people with whom we share our lives. It's like learning how to ride a bicycle without training wheels. At first we're always falling to one side or the other. Gradually we find balance, more quickly each time. Eventually, balance feels natural.

We need to be gentle with ourselves and others as we begin our quest for balance. I found that my friends, family, and co-workers were often unaccepting of my new attitude. They were confused by the turnaround from my previous behavior. I swung from one extreme to the other. One minute I was aggressive and demanding; the next minute I was compliant and excessively agreeable.

One technique that helped me find balance was to experiment with people outside my usual social circles. I went to a department store and politely asked a salesperson to help me find an item I wished to buy. Before I started recovery, I would have bought merchandise from a salesperson who intimidated me through their attitude or their neglect of me as a customer. I would, literally, buy into that demoralizing routine because I accepted people putting me down all of the time. Now, I asked probing questions about the quality of the particular item, where it was made, what the warranty was, anything I cared to know.

The greatest benefit of that exercise for me was that finally I took some control in a situation. If I wasn't satisfied with the service I received, or if the merchandise didn't suit me, I took control and chose not to buy anything from that clerk. If I was happy with their service, I purchased the item, and felt good giving my money to the clerk.

I learned how to be assertive in gaining information. I accepted giving (my money) and taking (the product *plus* service) in a functional way. Eventually, I was able to use this skill with my friends, family, and co-workers with confidence.

You can try this technique yourself. I think you will be surprised how much you can gain from it. We *can* learn to use appropriate ways of being assertive without the risk of confrontation that haunts us all when we first start standing up for ourselves. We can also learn how to be comfortable making requests of people, as well as drawing boundaries in situations when another person is wrongfully taking power away from us.

In recovery, we learn balance by learning to be fair with ourselves as well as others.

25. LEARNING TO TRUST ME

I had relied on others for my identity and sense of self for so long I didn't really trust my own decisions. I had told myself for so long that I was stupid (something I learned growing up) that I believed it. So learning to trust me was quite an adventure.

To help me in this process, a friend gave me the song "Singing in the Rain." I used the umbrella as a shield to help me visualize boundaries by imagining it as my God-brella. When it was time to decide what to make for dinner, instead of asking the family, I decided, and the wrath that I expected to follow when I made decisions was bounced off the umbrella. Oh, I didn't really have an actual umbrella, but I imagined one of soft glowing pink light filled with love. And when the complaints like, "Oh, not meat loaf, you know I hate that!" came toward me, I hummed my song and turned my umbrella toward that person to let God's love handle it. I trusted that I had planned a good, tasty dinner.

It helped me not to take the comments personally. It helped me let others have likes and dislikes without having my whole identity crushed. It helped me learn to have boundaries and to trust my decisions for me without feeling guilty.

For so long I believed that I didn't deserve to make decisions. The umbrella gave me a way to smile to myself as I hummed, "I'm happy again." I visualized the rainwater washing away my fear of not being liked and the old ways of thinking and reacting. I visualized splashing in puddles as taking responsibility for my life and learning to act instead.

It seemed like a childish kind of exercise, but I loved it. It helped me keep my sense of humor and not take others or myself so seriously. It helped me learn to trust me by giving me a chance to be trusted.

26. PATTERNS

For years, all my relationships followed the same pattern: I would become involved with someone who "needed" me, and throw my whole self into taking care of their needs. I always fell for the guys who were out of work, out of money, and needed a place to live. I would take them in, feed them, support them until they found a job, bolster their egos, smother them with affection, and then cry myself sick when they left me, telling me they needed "space." I was a one-woman Salvation Army!

When I started recovery, I began to understand why I let these patterns rule my life. My father, an alcoholic, died when I was eleven. He had had a bad heart and a collapsed lung for as long as I could remember. My mother was the "strong one" of my parents, and did everything for the family. She worked full-time, ran the house, and reared four children, pretty much by herself. Dad needed a lot of care, and his wishes were always deferred to by the rest of us. He controlled our emotional lives with an iron hand.

By working the Steps, I'm beginning to make changes for the better in my relationships. The honesty required by the Program has made me realize that I can't keep playing out the same old tapes. I have to change *my* attitudes and beliefs if I want the patterns to change.

27. THE CHILD WITHIN

Little girl inside of me
I'm surprised that you're still there
Patiently waiting for me to see
How much you need my care

Little girl, your tears are felt
They fall upon my own face
And all that pain that you've been dealt
I wish I could erase

Little girl, I'll understand
If you can't trust me just now
But it's possible I've found a plan
To work this out somehow

Little girl, I'm going to hear
All the things you need from me
And from now on I'll hold you near
With love eternally

Little girl, your fear I feel
I wish I could make it subside
But that's the price for being real
And I'm just as scared inside

Little girl, a world's out there
Let's go see it together
Let's think of things that we can share
And pray it lasts forever.

28. TARGET

I grew up believing that God loved other people,
and I believed He could and would love me, if only I
weren't such a bad little girl. Oh, it wasn't that I was
bad all of the time, but I thought that it was inevitable
that anything I did would turn bad, like a giant water
balloon just waiting to hit me again. The nursery
rhyme seemed to say it all: "There once was a girl
who had a little curl right in the middle of her fore-
head. And when she was good, she was very, very
good, and when she was bad, she was horrid." That
was me. The very, very good part was when I did
things *your* way, my parents' way, or the Sunday
school teacher's way. When I did things *my* way, I
was doomed.

The trouble with being the water balloon target was that it splashed on whoever was around me. I knew that I should suffer (I was bad), but when you suffered that really upset me. I learned a way of survival (no, it was not life) that set me up to be a constant victim. I took my direction from how others were feeling. I valued everyone else's ideas over my own. I had no value, unless I was being a recipient of pain for others. I should suffer so at least someone could have happiness.

Knowing that God knew everything, and that I was bad, made working the Steps difficult. On the one hand I couldn't understand why giving my life over to the care of God would work. I thought I had done that years ago, and that was why I took the role of target. I thought God wanted me to be the one who sacrifices everything so everyone else could do good and have a happy life. Now I was being asked to do it again, and I couldn't see that it would be any different this time.

So I gave myself this assignment: visualize three water balloons and practice juggling them, one day at a time. When I missed one balloon, I called on a fellow recovering codependent and we talked about the miss. As you probably guessed by now, I used each balloon to represent a Step. Even though my balloons still continued to break, now I could be a target for the *solution.* As the water from my imaginary balloons splashed on others, it gave me an opportunity to be a part of the WE in Step One. Instead of my old way of thinking that I spread the pain of disease to those around me, I could think of spreading the joy of recovery with each splash.

Sharing what I was feeling, whether it seemed good or bad, was sharing me—the real me. This was living the Steps. This was admitting that WE worked, and that I trusted the process.

29. MADE A DECISION

As I sat across from my sponsor to begin studying Step Three, she peered at me and asked how I had gotten to the coffee shop. "Now, be specific," she told me. "Well," I began, "I left the house, got in my car, and drove here." "To understand Step Three," she said, "we'll start there. How did you leave your house?" Without giving me a chance to answer her, she continued, "You thought about it, and you chose a behavior, and you acted on it. We can apply the same to Step Three. You have thought about it in Step Two, and chosen the pathway of belief in God as you understand God, and Step Three is simply the action of your thoughts."

This simple explanation helped me, but of course I wanted it to be more complicated. As if anticipating my resistance, my sponsor continued with a second example. "It's as if you're thinking about turning left. You can resolve to do it, promise to do it, tell others that it's what you're going to do, but if you made a decision to do it, you imply that you have combined your resolve, thinking, and have already taken action. You have made (past tense) the decision. It's done, and it is not ever undone. You may fall into denial and think it's done, but once you have decided, that's it."

30. TURN IT OVER

Having already learned that this part of the action in Step Three meant letting go **and** letting God, we went directly to what *will* and *lives* meant. My sponsor explained that "will" was from the most powerful action verb around, "to be." I learned from her that this verb held the essence of the creative nature of man. That will was my motivation, my sense of direction, my value system, and my whole thinking structure.

Lives, she said, meant the extermination of will. This meant the actions, the physical attributes of my life. This also included my seemingly unasked for experiences that made me think I was a victim of others' behavior and the whole universe at times. "Lives" referred to what I was willing, or not willing, to allow in my life. Seeing my resistance rising, she said, "You don't have to understand this all at once, just be willing. That will be enough to begin the process of Step Three."

The trust I had learned while working Step Two began to take hold in Step Three. I did not yet understand everything my sponsor said, but as we talked, I knew I was willing, and a wonderful sense of serenity and hope glimmered inside me.

31. THE CARE OF GOD

The final section of Step Three was crucial, my sponsor said. She pointed out that I was *not* turning my will and life over to God, but over to the *care* of God. She wanted me to understand that the responsibility was still on me. This was why I had free will. I was free to choose, and now I knew what to choose in order to find the freedom from codependency that had eluded me my whole life.

She also pointed out that, one day at a time, my understanding of God may change, so I needed to check every day what my understanding was, so I knew what direction I should turn. I immediately protested, saying, "How would I know?" Almost before I had the words out, I saw her lips forming the word "Practice!" and we both laughed.

This Step was going to be both easier and harder than I thought. Easier, in that it all seemed so simple and the changes required of me would be God-directed. Harder, in that it really meant God was going to direct me now. I had a new pathway. I had committed to this new way, and somewhere inside, even though I was scared, a voice said, "Welcome."

32. LIVING STEP THREE

My sponsor gave me a small house plant and told me to care for it. She told me to write down every day what I did. I decided that little plant was going to grow to be the best, biggest plant alive. Within a week, it had yellow leaves. I felt like a failure, and worse, I had to tell my sponsor at our weekly meeting the results of my care. I cried. She laughed. "Only God knows how to perfectly care for all living things," she said.

She talked to me about my relationship to God and the plant. She said that I could trust God to know whatever I *needed* to continue to grow and stay healthy as long as I let him care for me. She also told me that God loved me so much that if I wanted to over-water plants, or anything else, God would let me, because this was a chance for me to learn. My attitude for such lessons should always be gratitude, if I wanted to experience the miracle of God working in my life.

She told me that when I had come to her, my attitude about the plant was one of fear, self-pity, and shame. She pointed out that these attitudes and feelings kept me from the solution. When I dwelt in these feelings, I was beating me up for not being God. She also told me that after we had talked and laughed about the plant I could be different. Thinking about her words, I did feel different. I felt a glow of gratitude. That little plant had been a teacher for me. I had learned that by saying "Thanks, God" instead of "poor me," I could hold my head up and not be ashamed of not being perfect. Being perfect was God's job. He was the boss. He was the one in charge.

33. THE PLANT SURVIVES

The second week of my house plant care seemed easier. I got direction at the plant store on how to care for my little yellow leaves and I started praying for direction from my Higher Power. My first week had been one of constant vigilance, but week two God put a newcomer in my life who needed rides to meetings.

All of a sudden the week was over and I had almost forgotten my plant. Running out the door to meet my sponsor, I made a quick check on it, and *we* had a new pale green leaf. I felt so proud! I couldn't wait to tell my sponsor.

Again, she laughed as I rattled on about being too busy to care for my plant. She reminded me of my grateful attitude. I agreed that I was grateful, but also proud. For what? she scolded me. Taken aback, I just let her talk. "Pride means you are taking credit. Let God have the credit. Be grateful. He got you busy so you didn't water it to death this week. He was directing this week. You let Him. You asked Him, too, and you went ahead and did the next thing in front of you all week."

I agreed it had been a fine week, and I also felt the difference between being grateful and being proud. Neither proud or ashamed, I could be grateful and trust that I was being directed, that God would use me to be of service to Him and to others if I stuck close to Him.

34. THE GOD BAG

The God Bag was my first action with boundaries. At first, that little brown paper grocery bag seemed like a pretty silly way to start looking at where

I started and others stopped, but it worked. I had actual anxiety attacks worrying about certain people. Well, really it was all people and their pets, and everything but me. As a result, I neglected me, ignored me, and was in total denial that I had any needs. I was miserable. With the God Bag, I began to experience a new sense of self.

I started paying attention to and watching for material to put "in the bag." My first entry was a newcomer who was *so* needy. I guess because she was part of the Program, I knew my sponsor would know if I took on her life as a project, so I put her in the bag and kept our relationship to my experience, strength, and hope. Boy, did I want to fix her! It would have been so simple, too (I thought). I talked to a couple of members about it and with their help I realized it was me I was trying to fix and the newcomer was none of my business. The feelings churning inside me were almost unbearable. I felt selfish and angry, less than, and queasy. I felt as if my heart was pounding right out of my chest, but I put her in the bag and each time I thought of her I said, "I don't have to handle her, she is in the bag."

It seemed like forever, going through the motions and putting an ever-increasing number of things in my God Bag, especially my family. I still loved them, but

I let God handle them. It was amazing how they responded. We got along.

At last I had made the transition. I was beginning to live a God-centered life. One day at a time, I had my work in front of me and everything else was in the bag. I began to see that even with my very best intentions, God handled the world better than I did. I was awestruck at how free I felt having my own life instead of having to run the world. I found a new sense of harmony when I put the world in the bag and told myself, "It's none of your business. Walk in your own shoes." I felt I had arrived in recovery.

35. PHONING GOD

My sponsor smiled and told me I didn't have to call her every day at the same time any more. Of course I *could* call, but now I only *had* to call once a week, or whenever I needed to. The reason, she said, was that now once a day, every day, I would call God and talk to my Higher Power in the way she and I had chatted, because now I had established a conscious contact with my Higher Power. It was my responsibility to call God, to nurture and maintain our relationship the way I had learned to do in recovery.

It was a sad time, but a joyful time. I felt I was really a part of the Program now. As I began to experience God's will, I learned the difference between my will and my Higher Power's will. It isn't always black and white. I don't always know right at the moment when I pray for guidance, but I discovered that as I continue to sincerely and humbly work Steps One, Two, and Three, I find that calm sense of security and serenity I so desperately sought my whole life. When I stop and pray for direction, and listen for answers, and then turn my thoughts to doing the next right thing, I have boundaries instead of walls. I know what is my business and what is none of my business. It doesn't seem to happen perfectly all the time, but that is how I learn to do it differently. It is a lifelong path and I am grateful to my Higher Power for being a part of it.

36. PRECIOUS CHILD

Precious and free were words used to describe others, or animals. I choked at applying them to me. I could agree with the concept of a child within. Sure, I had glimpses of the playful part of me and the demanding part of me, even the angry part who stamped her foot like a two-year-old. But the idea that I was to get all gooey and call myself precious and free was abhorrent to me.

My fellow members advised me to share my feelings at meetings and I did. There were some who laughed, some who avoided me, and some who ignored me. Several people shook their heads and looked sad. Two people approached me after the meeting. I expected some sort of lecture, but they just invited me out for coffee. Coffee, that is, at the local miniature golf place. Nothing was said about any inner child stuff. They just played and laughed and talked to me about their lives.

At the next meeting, I felt I had two new friends. After the meeting, they again invited me to coffee. This time it was at the bowling alley. I shared about how lonely I had felt as a kid, sitting and watching my dad bowl and not feeling big enough or good enough to bowl with him. They shared similar stories. We all laughed about it. We also said we were glad we were free of those restraints. The thing was, though, that I didn't feel free. I felt really angry.

As I related the outing to my sponsor, she questioned me about feeling angry. No, I wasn't mad at my new friends. No, I was enjoying bowling, up until we had reminisced. As gently as I have ever heard her, she said, "Oh, honey, that was your inner child. She didn't feel precious or free, did she?" I was stunned. Of course she didn't. She was never those things. "She can be now," my sponsor said, and became very quiet waiting for me to respond.

My heart was in my throat and my head hummed. I wanted to scream, "No, she can't. She is not allowed to." All I could do was sob. For the first time I could see the twisted, tired, earnest little girl I had been and continued to be, taking responsibility for actions and attitudes that were my parents', teachers', family's, and everyone's but hers. She was so immature, she was so sad. I felt so helpless.

Tears rolled down my cheeks. Where do I start? I thought to myself. At the beginning, Step One. As the word "we" jumped into my mind, I reached out and held my sponsor's hand. The word "powerless" came into my mind and it gave me the courage to look up into my sponsor's loving face. She nodded as I mouthed the word. Powerless. Yes, I knew that I didn't know. I knew that I needed help. I knew that I wanted help. Most importantly, for the first time, I knew that I deserved help. It was mine for the taking.

The tears gave way to a shy smile. As we sat in silence, I was finally able to ask, "What do I do?" "Gently," my sponsor said, "Listen, share, write, work the Steps. You are not alone, precious child. You are part of a group of wounded children learning to be free. Practice what is offered to you. You will find your way."

37. MINDING MY OWN BUSINESS

One of the first things I heard after getting into recovery was that I must learn to deal with only those problems which are mine.

To me, this was a polite way of saying, "Mind my own business." Since it has always been my nature to feel that I know what is best for everyone, deciding what is my business and what is *not* has been extremely difficult.

Although we are provided with numerous slogans as tools, I could not find one which quite seemed to fit for this glaring defect of mine.

I decided that perhaps I could devise some personal tools of my own which would help. I came up with two questions which force me to look honestly at myself when I feel the urge to give unsolicited advice or to otherwise become involved in things which do not concern me:

(1) Is that your problem?

(2) Did anyone ask your opinion?

It's amazing how frequently the answer to both of these questions is NO!

This keeps my Program simple and helps keep me comfortable in recovery.

38. MANAGING MONEY

Money itself is powerless until we take possession of it. It is, arguably, the most manipulated inanimate object that humankind has ever created. Through this massive manipulation, we created Greed, and have associated money with power ever since.

Having control of your money can be a very empowering feeling. Many of us, over the course of our codependent journeys, have given this power away to others—particularly to our partners. We let them convince us that we are incapable of managing money. Thus, we become powerless over financial affairs, and consequently more dependent on them. This puts us in a vulnerable situation. Money can't buy us love, but it *can* buy us freedom if we're in a desperate situation.

Every household's financial situation is their own business, but we can make our contribution our business. We can take an active interest in what's going on with the checkbook, savings, and investments. If we employ a professional financial planner or bookkeeper, we can make certain that their interests are non-partial to all members of our household.

Learning to manage money isn't easy. It is a matter of observing and controlling our spending habits. Free and inexpensive courses are available through experimental colleges and extension colleges. A good book to read is *How to Get Out of Debt, Stay Out of Debt, and Live Prosperously*, by Gerrold Mundis, published by Bantam Books.

Managing our own money is one of the most empowering things we can do for ourselves. It is much less scary to know the facts than to guess. Money is one of the tools that assists us in shaping our future in recovery.

39. CHAMELEON

In the days before recovery, I was an expert at protective coloring. I hid myself behind a false face, and pretended to be whatever other people wanted me to be. You wanted to be smarter than I am? Presto, I was the original "dumb blonde." You wanted me to be outgoing? Abracadabra, I was a "party girl." You wanted a casual involvement, with no commitments? Gosh, stable relationships are so boring!

Chameleons had nothing on me. I could change "color" at a moment's notice, as soon as I had an idea what you wanted to see. My true self was buried beneath so many layers, I had no idea who she was.

Recovery has given me the tools to dig her out. Every day, one day at a time, I learn a little more about her. The miracle is, I've discovered she's a pretty nice person just as she is!

40. LISTEN TO THE MUSIC

Most of us remember learning the ABC's in song. We may even have learned to recite the states of the union in song—alphabetically, no less. Stop a moment to think about it. Without a melody, these words would be hard to learn in sequence. Mindlessly we can sing the ABC's, and many other songs that can be, unfortunately, degrading to our self-esteem.

Many "Top 40" songs of both today and yesteryear can be harmful to us as codependents if we accept the lyrics as acceptable actions. They talk about unreciprocated love, control, helplessness, and other dysfunctional behaviors. Every time we hear such lyrics, they imprint our minds much deeper than common logic can touch. This process is compounded when we sing along. When I think of how many songs I have stashed in my head, and all I have to do is hear the music to recite literally hundreds of songs, word for word—it is scary!

If I uttered some of those lyrics as spoken word, in simple conversation, I would send myself back to treatment. I'm not saying that music, or any sector of it, is bad. Music is a gift to us, but we should be careful how we hear it.

Listen to the lyric of the songs on your radio. Listen to yourself sing along. What are you singing? Then turn off your radio and think about the words you sang. Do you like those words? Do you find yourself making pictures in your mind of your own life experiences? I sure do. Just realize what is happening. Consciously decide what to keep in your head and what to dismiss. Think of it as a game. Music is fun. The lyrics are fantasy. They are not real, but YOU ARE. So take care of yourself, and listen to the music.

41. ACCEPTING HAPPINESS

I think the hardest assignment I've ever had in recovery is convincing myself it's O.K. to be happy. I never thought I deserved to be happy. I set myself up so I couldn't be, in everything from relationships to jobs. I slaved away, telling myself this was what life was all about, that it was supposed to be drudgery. Having fun was sinful; giving yourself pleasure was giving in to weakness. All of us, and me especially, were "bad" from birth and must be taught to be "good" through hard work and duty. Neglect of either of these was the ultimate "bad."

In recovery, I've learned that I'm not good or bad, only my actions and reactions are. I've learned that happiness is a normal state of being, not a path to the devil. I deserve it; I am worthy of it; and one day at a time, I'm learning to enjoy it.

42. I DIDN'T HAVE TIME

I got up early one morning
And rushed right into the day;
I had so much to accomplish
That I didn't have time to pray.

Problems just tumbled about me
And heavier came each task;
"Why doesn't God help me," I wondered.
He answered, "You didn't ask."

I wanted to see joy and beauty
But the day toiled on, gray and bleak.
I wondered why God didn't show me.
He said, "But you didn't seek."

I tried to come into God's presence;
I used all my keys at the lock.
God gently and lovingly chided,
"My child, you didn't knock."

I woke up early this morning
And paused before entering the day.
I had so much to accomplish
That I had to take time to pray.

43. LOOSE ROCKS

I have always believed that when I was asked a question, I was supposed to answer, in detail, to the fullest extent of my knowledge. The only secrets I kept were when someone told me not to tell. I needed to tell everything. In fact, if I remembered something I had left out, I would interrupt to fill in the blanks. It was my duty.

My Fourth Step inventory gave me the window I needed to look at my behavior. My first awarenesses told me I had an exceptional gift to anticipate what everyone wanted to know, thereby giving them such excellently detailed information. I looked at this quality as a rare asset, one that more people needed to develop.

As I looked further I found that I really had very few friends. Many people considered me a know-it-all. I knew I had many life experiences that did give me knowledge, but why did I put people off so, when others attracted friends?

This dilemma carried into my Fifth Step, and here I could finally see that others didn't ignore me, I pushed them away. By going back to my family lifestyle and looking at how my family communicated, I found I had learned to dump information on people.

"Why didn't you tell me?" was frequently screamed at my house. "If I had known the details, I wouldn't have been so mad," was the message I heard. So becoming the perfect storyteller was a survival tool I learned as a child, and I carried it into adulthood where it no longer helped me, but got in my way. The results were constant feelings of fear, anger, frustration, and inferiority. I had no intimacy in my life. I was either a victim or a victimizer. I had no other roles.

I set myself up to be hurt by giving information about myself to people who had no capacity to respect me. I had no tools for looking where I was going. Like a hiker on the trail of life, I stepped on loose rocks and fell, and then cried, "Stupid rock!" I crossed streams on shaky bridges, fell in, and blamed the bridge. I failed to use my innate sense of protection because I had learned to ignore and discount it.

I wanted to deny it—no, this can't be true. I felt a heartache that strangled me. I had tried so very hard for so very long to tell everything, to be a good girl, to trust everyone, and now I was finding out that it was my responsibility to choose, that I had to be responsible for my feelings. I couldn't blame someone else. How powerfully I had set them up to victimize me!

As I wrangled with these feelings, I went back through Steps One, Two, and Three. I also had the hope of the Steps to come, which explain how we clean up the wreckage of our past. I listened, read, and prayed, asking for God's help.

As I prayed, I began to feel as if I had a whole new world to explore. I was scared, but I was not alone. There would be times when I still chose loose rocks to step on, but I could and would learn as I went if I kept close to my Higher Power.

44. PRAYER IS A SPECIAL TIME

Prayer is a special time I share with God. Prayer is the means I use to talk with God and to listen as God communicates with me. When I pray, I become still and quiet any unrest within me. I reaffirm my oneness with my Higher Power and I find the answers I seek.

I do not limit my prayers to a certain time or a particular place. Whenever a small success enters my life or a moment of joy illuminates my day, I silently thank God for those blessings. Every time I affirm God as the source of my good and give thanks for the many channels through which it comes, I am praying to God.

Prayer enables me to know and to feel that I am a beloved child of God. I am needed because I can be an expression of good in my world.

45. ENDINGS VS. BEGINNINGS

I rarely could look at any of life's experiences as an opportunity for a new beginning. I always concentrated on the ending and hated for it to happen, whether it was good or bad. I hung onto relationships that should have ended, worked at jobs too long, and refused to give up on "old ideas" (still do some of the time).

Even when I started something new, I projected the end; and it was never going to be good.

The Program tells me that I must close a door so that a new door will open. But I hesitate doing so, because I want to know what's behind the new door before risking it.

Whenever something ended, it seemed like the end of the world to me. I am slowly becoming aware that it "ain't necessarily so."

It's a relief to find out that I can fail at something and that doesn't have to be the end. I can start all over, make a new beginning. I ordinarily wouldn't even start if I thought I was doomed to fail. Today, I try not to project "the end" and work at whatever I am doing just for today.

Endings don't frighten me today like they used to, because I am starting to realize for every ending there will be a new beginning.

46. CHANGES

When I married, no one had even heard the word "codependent," let alone defined it. I married an alcoholic, who had been battered as a child. When drunk, he carried on that conditioning with me, and later with our son.

I had been reared to believe that a "good wife" was loyal, dutiful, and submissive to her husband, and that marriage was forever, no matter what. It was my job to make it work, whatever it cost. It took me ten years and a lot of heartache to break those beliefs. I

swore I would never get involved with anyone like my
ex-husband again. I felt I was a total failure. I had not
lived up to what I was "supposed" to do. Surely there
was something else I could have done to make him
quit drinking? After all, I had driven him to the bottle.
He told me so.

For years, every relationship I had followed the
same dismal pattern. No matter how carefully I chose
my partners, they all turned out very similar to my ex-
husband, even the ones who didn't drink. I couldn't
figure out what I was doing wrong. Why did I always
pick losers?

One evening, after I had been in recovery for
awhile, I was reminiscing with my mother, and she
told me a couple of stories about my dad that could
have come straight out of my marriage. I was stunned.
As far as I could remember, I had never seen my father drink. He was my hero—frail, sickly, and never
without an oxygen tank nearby, but still a giant to a
loving little girl. When he died just before I entered
my teens, I was devastated. Now I discovered, thirty
years later, that the man I had worshipped was an alcoholic.

The light bulb went off, and I began to remember
things I had buried deep in my subconscious. It was
as if the pattern of my whole life changed colors. I
began to understand.

My true recovery began at that point, and every day I am getting better. I know now that I don't have to keep playing out the same roles time after time. I can let my father go, and forgive him for leaving me.

47. MAY WE GO FORTH

May we go forth to the duties of our days, with willing hands and honest minds, with faith in the power of good over evil, ready to take our places in the world.

We shall expect to be forgiven only as we forgive others,

Working and hoping for that day when ties of brotherhood and sisterhood shall bind together every member of the human family.

—George Rudolph Freeman
(adapted)

48. OLD TIMERS NEED SUPPORT TOO

Sometimes at a meeting, I feel like I cannot or should not "share" because I am going through a difficult time myself. During those times I feel as if someone with as much time in recovery as I have should be an authority of sorts. I imagine my meeting friends looking at me as if asking me to say something profound. I take on the responsibility of being the

Perfect Role Model, when no one asked me to perform such a part. No such person exists, but I find myself striving to become that person anyway.

I beat myself up, grilling Me with such insensitive questions as "why aren't you more together today?" What's worse is that I can let myself slip back into that submissive role with my own ego suppressing me. If all of this sounds as codependent to you as it does to me, then you will understand that it is times such as these that Old Timers need a meeting more than ever! We need to hear that all codependents have troubles sometimes, regardless of how long we have been confronting our problems.

Once an alcoholic, always an alcoholic; once a codependent, always a codependent. Just as an alcoholic can quit drinking and work the Program, we codependents can identify and limit our codependent behaviors through working the Program. Regardless of how much time we have in recovery, we all need to support one another. Meetings are not just for newcomers. Old Timers need support, too.

49. BORN TO PLEASE

I was "born to please." I learned very early how to win praise from my parents by being a "good boy," especially compared to my older brother, who wasn't.

I had to work hard to please my folks. Nothing was ever good enough. I coped by pretending to be whoever they wanted me to be. I was a robot, programmed to automatically ignore my own needs and please those around me.

As I grew older, I continued my people-pleasing with friends, family, co-workers, and associates. I felt empty and confused, and it just kept getting worse. Finally, I went to a counselor. He directed me to CoDA.

I began to find ways to express my feelings. I started keeping a journal. I spent more time alone, thinking and remembering. I discovered that some of my negative feelings were connected to old childhood fears and shame.

I'm learning to trust and respect my own needs and emotions. I'm learning to be present in the moment.

50. LEARNING TO BE A FRIEND

I never realized how difficult it is to be a friend. For years I tried to control every relationship I was in, and I smothered anyone I called friend. It has been hard to let go of that tendency.

I always had only one friend at a time, and I thought that person had to be *my* friend exclusively.

To be called "one of my friends" by someone to whom I gave all my attention felt like a slight to me. After all, this person was *my* only friend, and I wanted sole rights to her friendship.

Thanks to two years in the Program I can see my errors. My exclusivity brought isolation. If my one and only friend wasn't available, I was alone. Now I have a network of beautiful, loving friends. As I reach out, I find that contact with others brings a new dimension to old relationships. I learn something from each person, and I become a better friend.

Still, I am sometimes apt to confuse love with smothering and stifling. There's the old urge to control people by "saving" them. If someone hurts, I have a band-aid; for every bad time, I have a solution.

It takes a great deal of effort not to try to run everyone's life, but I'm working at it. Daily, I ask God's help in releasing my friends to the care of their Higher Power.

A true friend listens without judging, helps without solving, loves without clinging. A friend has a number of interests and engages in a variety of activities that serve to enliven a friendship. A friend is there when needed, but respects the other's need for privacy.

There is something almost mythically idealistic about this portrait of a friend. I may never reach that ideal, but I am trying my best, and that's all I can do. Recovery calls for progress, not perfection.

51. C.O.P.E.

People-pleasing was a work of art for me. I was better at it than anyone—the best hostess, the friend, always there for you, the "good Samaritan." The trouble was that this skill of mine was killing me.

When my therapist sent me to CoDA, I was shocked to find that people-pleasing was at the core of codependency and low self-esteem. I found out that I did things to make people like me because I felt so worthless I thought they wouldn't love me unless I bent over backward for them. I also found out that most of my resentments were based on demands that others bend over backward for me.

In recovery from codependency, I've learned that I can and must do things to please *me*. My responsibility is to walk in my own shoes and *do* for me. When I do for you, it is because I want to for me, not because I am trying to manipulate you into liking me, and not because I am trying to feel worthy. When I do for others, it's not so people will say, "Look at her;

she is such a good person," it's so I can say to myself, "I like me."

The Program gave me "C.O.P.E." (Cut Out Pleasing Everyone). My instructions were to think that if I am trying to cope with a situation, I am people-pleasing. If I am C.O.P.E.ing with the situation, I am taking care of me first. This way I can live the principles of recovery: responsibility, honesty, and willingness. Living in principle creates healthy boundaries. These boundaries help me honor myself and give me self-esteem—doing the right thing for the right reason.

Trusting in myself gives me the understanding and trust in my Higher Power that my actions will be out of love for the other person, not out of trying to get them to love me. I become less self-centered and free to have healthy relationships. I recover from codependency.

52. BLAME AS A BLOCK TO RECOVERY

As long as I blame others, circumstances, and past events for my present situation, I am not accepting my own responsibility; and therefore, no growth or change can occur.

Blame is the way we humans shrug off responsibility for things occurring in our lives. By continually blaming, I refuse to look at the contributions my behaviors make to the situation; and therefore, I do nothing to change. As I give reason after reason for things not going the way I like, I keep myself from looking inward and choosing what I can do to change whatever is making me unhappy. Even laying guilt trips on my parents, spouse, or children does nothing to really alter my unhappiness. I have adapted to living with someone who has consistently disappointed, humiliated, angered and disgusted me. I have blamed, cajoled, supported, and defended the chemically dependent. I have questioned my judgment in choosing to remain in contact with a person who is "weak" and simultaneously I have feared my own inadequacies. I have rationalized my relationship with that person just as she has rationalized using.

Blaming another keeps me a slave; I am helpless in another's hands since my feelings become the responsibility of someone else. I will never be in charge of my own person if I choose to turn that control (blame) over to another. Blaming closes me to feedback because I rationalize why I am "right" and the other is "wrong," and I choose not to listen to what I label as "wrong."

If another is blamed for, or accepts responsibility for, my failures, then that person must also be credited for my successes, and vice versa, and this reduces that individual to non-personhood.

The only way to get out of this trap is to stop blaming. I refuse to let myself complain, find fault, or accuse another for my frustrations, sadness, and lack of a satisfying lifestyle. This process will take effort and practice, for old habits are difficult to break; but once I recognize that blaming another keeps me from participating wholly in life, I will find that my family, friends, and others close to me will help restore me to sanity. (One suggestion for working on new behaviors is to announce that I wish to get rid of this shortcoming and that I want those around me to signal me when I fall in the trap again.)

I know that every new bit of growth takes effort and concentration until it becomes a part of my life. Relationships don't get better in and of themselves. It takes commitment and effort. Communications long couched in mutual blame-laying must be replaced with the ability to say how I feel and to accept responsibility for my feelings without laying the cause of them on another. By using "I" in stating my thoughts, sensory experience, feelings, intentions, and actions, instead of "You," "We," and "Us," I take responsibility for myself and allow others to take responsibility for themselves.

Before I can accept my powerlessness in dependency, as the dependent or codependent, I need to eliminate blame from my thoughts, attitude, and communications. Only then will I be able to be responsible in my relationships.

Responsibility, then, is the ability to fulfill my needs, and to do this in a way that does not deprive others of the ability to fulfill their needs.

53. IMAGE

"What will the neighbors think?" This was my mother's overriding concern when I was growing up, and for years I agonized over the image I presented to other people.

My husband was perfect—at least I told everyone he was. My children never did anything wrong—as far as anyone outside our immediate family knew. I had a perfect life—and I was slowly dying because I felt so empty and alone. I was desperate for help. I found it when I walked into these rooms.

Everyone was so open about all the things I'd tried to hide for so long! I was amazed. Some of them had much worse problems than any I had had. I began to understand how I had let others' opinions and beliefs control my life and keep me trapped in dishonesty and game-playing.

Through recovery, I'm gradually gaining a sense of who I really am. I'm learning to like the real me. Every day, the "image" I see in the mirror is coming closer to my true self.

54. EXCUSES

My recovery has helped me in many ways. Today I've been thinking about what a change I've made in my attitude around the subject of excuses. Before the Program, I used my differences as excuses. Because I wasn't good-looking enough, tall enough, rich enough, smart enough, I could get away with or not try certain things. My thinking and attitude limited my behavior and at the same time caused me to act out in negative and strange ways.

They say that the Program is "education without graduation." I've learned that escaping from reality causes more problems than trying to cooperate with life. Reality is different and difficult at times, but I now know I can't change the *facts* of life that are out of my control. I *can* change my *attitudes* toward them. It simply comes down to working on acceptance.

I've slowly been able to remove the chip on my shoulder. I work at the Program every day and remember that problems don't come my way because "life isn't fair." It's important to our recovery to remember, "We don't have attitudes; they have us." I'm learning new attitudes toward old problems, and new solutions for them, by working my Program. I am learning to live in the real world.

55. PETS

Pets can be a joy to anyone, but to codependents for different reasons.

Growing up in a codependent environment, many of us lacked unconditional love from either or both parents. It is an empty, hollow feeling that is created from this type of situation. Our parents had the habit of only expressing their love and affection towards us when we pleased them. This is a terrible way to learn love, intimacy, and equality in relationships. Pets give unconditional love that can warm our hearts and embrace our souls. Their anticipation of our return home for the evening, taking walks together, or simple playtime are all examples of mutual caring that are beneficial to us along our codependent journey.

From a different light, it is appropriate to control pets. Owning a pet that is not properly licensed, a menace to neighbors or landlords, is emulating that pattern of neglect and irresponsibility.

I had a difficult time with my first pet after I started working the CODA Program. I spent an excessive amount of time with my dog, to the point that I alienated everyone else. My dog is a good listener and sometimes I talked to him instead of the person involved! That wasn't healthy, either.

All in all, pets are faithful companions. With proper care, they will offer you unconditional love, perhaps for the first time in your life.

56. WHAT MOM TAUGHT ME

A lot of our codependent behaviors stem from the modelling we saw as children. Mom was, in most cases, our primary caretaker. We learned from her how to "take care of" others.

Even though we are "big kids" now, and can take care of our daily functions, there are still those certain things that we have implanted in our minds that "Mom does best." I don't mean that we expect *our* Mom to do them. I mean that now many of us are mothers, and we expect *ourselves* to be everything mothers "should be."

My Mom did all the housework and prepared three meals every single day for her family. She took care of wardrobe maintenance, did volunteer work, nurtured relationships with the neighbors, and supervised all us children during non-school hours. The list went on and on.

In this country, we have created a game called "Keeping Up With the Joneses." Society has determined that consuming more high-priced gadgets is necessary to maintain our standard of living. To achieve that standard, we have to increase family income by 50% or more. As a result, dual income households have become the norm today.

Society still expects women to do everything we did when we were home all day, plus work full-time, plus commute. That's terribly unfair to us, and self-defeating. There truly is not enough time in a day to do everything we "should" do. I saw a newspaper article a couple of years ago that made a list of all the things we think we should do, and how much time each of them "should" take. It would take 30 hours a day!

As responsible members of society, we must stop these great expectations, in ourselves and others. We must forgive ourselves and our neighbors for not doing *everything*. We must make choices.

Some activities and possessions may be cut from our own agendas. We need to embrace only those traditions which are meaningful to us, not just the ones which are habitual. We can free ourselves from the guilt, and take on new traditions which enhance our lives. We can season these with spontaneity. We can compose our own symphony of life, balancing the treble and the bass, melody and harmony, phrases and rests.

57. I AM

1.   I am a unique and precious human being, always doing the best I can, always growing in wisdom and love.

2.   I am in charge of my own life.

3.   My first responsibility is my own growth and well-being. The better I am to me, the better I will be to others.

4.   I refuse to be put down by the attitudes or opinions of others.

5.   My actions may be good or bad, but that doesn't make me good or bad.

6.   I make my own decisions and assume the responsibility of any mistakes. I need not feel shame about them.

7.   I am not free as to the things that will happen to me, but I am 100 percent free as to the attitude I have

toward these things. Whether I feel a sense of well-being or suffer depends on my attitude.

8. I do not have to prove myself to anyone. I need only express myself as honestly and effectively as I am capable.

9. I can be free of resentment.

10. My emotional well-being is dependent primarily on how much I love me.

11. I am kind and gentle toward me.

12. I live a day at a time, do first things first.

13. I am patient and serene for I have the rest of my life in which to grow.

14. Every experience I have in life, even the unpleasant ones, contributes to my learning and growth.

15. No one in the world is more important than I am.

16. My mistakes and failures do not make me a louse, a crumb, or whatever. They only prove that I am imperfect, that is, human. And there's nothing wrong with being human.

17. Once I have reconciled to God and my neighbor, I can be completely free of remorse.

58. CONFIDENCE

Simply getting started in working out codependent behaviors is one of the greatest challenges a person can ever face. The beginning can feel dark. It seems that it would be easier, less clumsy, to get a momentum going if we could start at a midway point. Confidence is what we need to see the light, to inspire ourselves, and get started. Our addiction has been working a long time destroying our personal confidence. Now we are reclaiming it, building it, and nourishing our self-esteem.

We start with acknowledging to ourselves what we do well. Any skill will do. All of us have talents that we take for granted and it is time that we validate ourselves for those wonderful things we do.

Maybe we have the cleanest kitchen on the block, or we are faithful recyclers. Perhaps we can change the oil in a car ourselves, or maybe we can knit a sweater. These are just a few examples of some skills that not everyone can or will do. There are a million talents like these and we perform thousands of them all of the time and don't even give ourselves credit for them. Think of it! We are fantastically talented!

For today, think of one, two, or ten of these talented skills that you perform. Then spend a few moments thinking about when you learned how to do each of these skills. Then spend a few moments thinking about how you refined each of them by doing them faster, better, or more efficiently. Compliment yourself. Tell yourself how much you appreciate having all those wonderful things done for you, your family and your friends for so many years. You will find that you are bright, skillful, and very accomplished!

59. CHAOS AND DRAMA

Although I didn't know it when I came to recovery, I soon learned that I was so used to crisis that I made everything a big deal. After spending the night with my sponsor, I had a crisis over which cereal to have for breakfast. It was a simple enough exclamation: "Oh, my goodness, how will I ever decide?" I had actually meant it as a compliment to the great choice available.

I settled on cereal and as we sipped our tea after breakfast, my sponsor pointed out my dramatics. She explained that crisis was what we wanted to avoid in recovery. (That is why we say the Serenity Prayer.) She mentioned that she had been observing me create crisis after crisis over others' problems, over everyday events, and when I got bored or things were getting peaceful. She shared her own experience, saying that as a newcomer and really on a day-to-day basis, she has had to learn to stop making mountains out of molehills.

As children, we live in chaotic surroundings. We become used to this. If it is a crisis, we can rush about so we don't have to feel. By creating crises, we can continue to feel the unmanageability we are accustomed to from childhood. Learning to build a serene life is new for most of us. Our extreme sensitivities lead to crisis and drama, but we can and do learn to live differently.

My sponsor suggested I learn to create boundaries which would enable me to feel what was going on around me without jumping into my "ain't it awful" or "oh, my God" modes. Reminding me that recovery is an inside job, she helped me create a safe place inside where I could practice going to get closer to my Higher Power and experience more serenity.

Of course, I was somewhat skeptical, but I knew it worked for her. That morning she shared her place with me. We went to a lovely English-style garden with hummingbirds and butterflies hovering around rainbows of flowers. Underfoot, we visualized warm wet earth, and above we created soft billowing clouds. Breathing together in silence, we listened to music and relaxed in the garden. Some time passed before I again became aware of lying on her couch. I felt serene.

She told me she had just introduced me to what she called "practicing the presence of God." She explained that this was an aspect of her daily meditation she had shared with me. She said I could create whatever was comfortable for me, but that it must be a peaceful, God-filled space. She told me that coming out of her garden reinforced her inner knowing that God was in charge and what seemed good or bad was just her own limited view. It was all in God's working and his vision far exceeded ours. Who, then, was I to be the judge, when it was not my job?

I didn't answer her question, but I got the message. At lunch when she offered me a choice of sandwiches, I stopped and breathed and chose. I thanked her for offering me a choice.

60. TAKING CARE AND CARETAKING

Growing up with axioms such as "do unto others," "you are your brother's keeper," "last is always best," "it is better to give than to receive," and my favorite, "mother's little helper," sets up a pattern of thinking to rationalize codependent behaviors. This thinking, combined with a family which has unmet emotional needs, leads to the trap of caretaking.

Being kind, loving, thoughtful, of service to your fellows, and recognizing others' needs is not bad, but when we neglect ourselves, it becomes unhealthy and can kill our spirits. Feelings of being taken advantage of or victimized, abused, or unappreciated are warning signs from ourselves to tell us that we are taking on responsibilities which may not belong to us. These warning signs frequently make us feel guilty and shamed, so we deny them and work even harder at doing for others. The cycle continues until we learn to listen to our own inner voices and start taking care instead of caretaking.

Anytime I consistently let my needs go unmet in order to meet the needs of another, I am cheating us both. I set the other person up to have unrealistic expectations of my capabilities. I set the other person up to victimize me. I rob myself of being me. This is the greatest dishonesty and disservice of codependency.

It feels good to help others, and it is. But helping others in lieu of feeling my feelings doesn't work. When the hungry man comes to me and asks for food, my codependency says, "Here, eat my fish and the kids' fish, too." Recovery has taught me that I am of greater service to the hungry man if I allow him self-respect and say, "Here, let me show you how to fish." In this way, the man will have a skill that allows him to eat for a lifetime.

Caretaking would have been a good emotional fix in my codependency. Oh, what pats on the back I could have given myself. But taking care, respecting the hungry man's boundaries, the kids' boundaries, and my own allowed us to experience responsibility. The man could learn to care for himself, and I could learn to care for us both.

61. CONTROL FREAK

I grew up feeling as if I never got my way. I am a twin, and what an excuse that is! As I got older, friends would say, "You're an Aries. Typically, you always think you're right." I hated that. I didn't always think I was right, did I?

As I look back, I know that I hated to go to places I had never been. I got anxiety attacks if I was invited to a function and didn't know exactly who would be there, how long it would last, what foods would be served, and every other detail. I wanted a "rundown" on people before I met them. I was afraid all the time and didn't know it. I wanted to know when my room-mates came and went and what they were doing. I felt left out a lot. I felt as if I still didn't get my way.

About seven months into recovery, I was on a plane trip with two friends. We had seats that faced one another, and it was fun. We were on our way to a recovery convention. I felt anxious about the trip and really didn't know I was at it again until one friend sighed and said, "O.K., you can be in charge. Is that what will make you settle down?" I was stunned. I realized I had "organized" who sat where, a game to play to keep us occupied. I dominated the conversation. It was true; I was controlling everything. I was afraid. I was also grateful.

Yes, I seemed like a control freak. In truth, whenever I felt afraid I took control. I was more of a fear freak.

I learned that growing up in an unpredictable environment had taught me that if I could take charge, I wouldn't feel so powerless. Controlling was my way of acting out my fear. It was my way of trying to have a balanced childhood. As a child, this skill had saved my life. Now it kept me in codependency and pushed people away from me.

To grow out of controlling, we learn to *be* instead of do. We sit and breathe and feel. When I do this my heart pounds, my stomach knots up, and I want to run, but it is easier now. I know how to be at a party and not run the show. I even enjoy it.

62. ROG OR ESH?

Filled with all the new information the Program offers, it is easy to fall into the old ways of codependency and rely on rumor, opinion, and gossip. Those old friends puff me up with a false sense of pride. I become a know-it-all. The worst part is I cheat me out of recovery and you too.

The character defects that lead me to rely on the old way are attractive. They give me a feeling of importance, but they aren't the way of recovery. Experience, strength, and hope are the way of recovery.

I was very good at telling everyone from the postman to the stranger on the street how to run their lives—Ms. Fix-it. My genuine caring for others and my habit of running from my own life were the perfect set-up. I offered opinions on things I didn't even understand.

In recovery I have learned to wait until someone asks. Then I can offer experience, strength, and hope. I have strength and hope because of the Twelve Steps, but if I don't have a similar experience to share, I pass. If I know someone with experience, I might suggest them, but I don't pass on opinion, rumor, and gossip. I don't break another's confidence by saying, "Oh, ask Sue. Didn't you know? She just got dumped, too."

I also offer my prayers. That is part of my experience.

To help me remember the difference, I have abbreviated Rumor, Opinion, and Gossip to ROG, and Experience, Strength, and Hope to ESH. ESH keeps me from MESH, the dangerous codependent relationships. ROG keeps me from GOD, the power of my understanding that runs the show. So ESH helps me step away from the disease into recovery. ROG makes me step away from recovery and into the disease.

If I am rogging, I know I am running away. If I'm eshing, I know I am bringing the solution to the situation. Rogging rhymes with jogging and eshing rhymes with fishing. When I fish, I get to eat and grow; when I jog I visualize escaping and missing out.

63. JUDGMENTAL

I worried constantly about how my husband and my children felt. I knew what was best for them, but they didn't listen to me. The more I tried to convince them my way was right, the more they withdrew from me.

If my daughter had a fight with a friend, I would call her friend's mother and fix it. If my son had trouble with his homework, I would do it for him. I wanted them both to be happy all the time—or at least act as if they were.

My husband finally talked me into going to family counseling. He wanted to be able to share his problems with me, and he saw how my constant worrying was hurting our children. In counseling, I began to see how my self-defeating behaviors were creating problems for me and my family. I joined a codependency recovery group.

One of the things that helped me most was keeping a journal. From my writings, I could see how often I sat in judgment on my husband and kids. I always knew what was best for them, and I kept trying to get them to see it my way.

With the help of my group and my journal, I traced my feelings back to childhood. My mother had spent a lot of time and energy trying to manage my father's alcoholism. I had been responsible for taking care of my brothers and sister from a very early age. I had learned to focus my attention on other people so I could run away from my strong and painful feelings.

At first I didn't want to admit I was so judgmental, but the truth was I didn't trust other people to know what was best for themselves.

Now, I bite my tongue when I want to give advice to my family. It was hard to trust God to make sure things turned out the way I wanted, but I began to see that sometimes my Higher Power has a better plan. These days, whenever I'm tempted to take care of other people, I ask myself what I need and concentrate on taking care of myself.

64. HOW ARE YOU?

Before recovery, there were no limits on what I would say. It was as if I would run up and throw up on people's shoes. "How are you?" they might ask, and I would respond with colorful accuracy about every ache and pain, or every reason why I was good or bad. I never gave people a chance to have a conversation because I told them everything in one breath. I robbed them of the chance to have boundaries because I didn't have any. This created walls. It was the only way people could keep me out; it was all or nothing with me.

I needed (I thought) other people so much. Without them I had no identity. My feelings, my moods, my life goals, were dependent on the person I was with. When I started recovery, I carefully limited the time I spent with any one person, because I was aware that I burned people out, but I never understood why.

Now the reason is clear. The person I needed so desperately to listen to, to love, to validate and respect was myself. I was flabbergasted that it was even an option. I had no idea that was how healthy people lived. I was learning how to walk through life as me, how to listen to the voice inside, and how to identify and respect my boundaries as well as others. It was a powerful promise, but I knew it was the truth. When fear comes, and it does, I ask God to remove it at once. If I did not, my lifelong skills would demand that I feed it, and it would grow. By asking that it be removed, I can go ahead with the assurance that God and I, together, can walk through it.

It is like a whole new mountain, a new trail, and a new guide. The view is fantastic. Now, when someone asks, "How are you?" I check my feelings and answer, "O.K."

65. WE GET WHAT WE WORK FOR

There is no magic in recovery. We get what we work for.

When I first came in, I wanted all the good things people had but I didn't want to work for them. Oh, I worked the Steps—at least the ones I thought I needed. And when it came to Steps 6 and 7, I was ready and willing to have my Higher Power remove my shortcomings—should I have any, of course. I had no idea what they were because I didn't think I needed Steps 4 and 5. But I prayed, vaguely, that should He see any shortcomings, I was ready for Him to remove them. The principle of Step 7 is humility. I had none.

As I made progress in recovery, I became aware of many character defects and of just how blind I had been to them. Mercifully, my Higher Power showed me only what I was ready to see.

I became depressed and thought I could never be forgiven for or relieved from these shortcomings. This depression, I discovered, was not humility, but another form of "playing God," believing my character defects were more powerful than my Higher Power's forgiveness.

Then, when I recognized Who had the power and who was powerless, I had to decide if I were "entirely ready" to ask Him to remove my shortcomings. After all, my character defects were what made up my personality, and I was pretty much in love with who I was. Self-will had been my HP for a lifetime. I was afraid, not knowing that something better would take the place of my character defects.

With all the honesty I was capable of at the time, I worked the Steps in order, 1 through 6, then 7, asking as humbly as I could that my Higher Power remove my shortcomings. They did not disappear. I was not struck pure.

Then I was made aware that character defects are like active codependency. I couldn't keep practicing my character defects and expect God to remove them.

I was going to have to develop a new set of habits—to work against myself—and as I practiced these new habits, the old habits/character defects would begin to die.

And so I began really living the Program, the daily striving to change, to let go and receive more. It doesn't happen overnight. It takes years of practice. I have not yet been struck pure. I am not a saint. But I claim, accept, and am grateful for spiritual progress.

66. WHAT IS SELF-ESTEEM, ANYWAY?

Cockiness, arrogance, knowing the right answer, feeling "better than," feeling worthy of attention, being proud: these were all the definitions I could think of when I tried to define self-esteem.

So I went to the dictionary: *self-esteem—belief in oneself; esteem—to have great regard for, highly value; self—the identity, character, or essential qualities of any person.*

A friend suggested I try this experiment: I had five index cards, numbered 1 through 5. I gave each card to someone in the Program and asked them to write down five characteristics they saw in me. This was very scary and uncomfortable for me, but I did it anyway.

With the information I gathered, my sponsor and I discussed my lack of self-esteem. I didn't know self-esteem was possible for me. I had spent so much of my life minimizing any accomplishments I had made and telling myself I wasn't enough. Even an A in school wasn't good enough; it should have been an A+. My esteem was based on how bad I was.

We combined the lists my friends in the Program had made. Under each characteristic I had to list three ways to honor that part of me. These had to be actions, statements, affirmations for me to say to myself. What a chore! What rewards!

I found out that I was responsible for building my own self-esteem. It wasn't something I had learned to do as a child, but I could learn to do it now. It was the beginning of honoring my self and my inner child. It was the beginning of my knowing where I needed boundaries. It was the beginning of freedom from codependency.

Self-esteem means honoring myself—all of me. It means nurturing and taking care of me. It means knowing who I am and being patient with me. It is listening to and following my inner voice. It is saying yes when I mean yes, and no when I mean no. Self-esteem feels good. It is still awkward at times, but I keep practicing. Self-esteem is not having to be perfect. Self-esteem is freedom to be me.

67. CHALLENGES

Letting go has always been one of my most difficult challenges. It has always been easier for me to tighten my grip than to enjoy the release of letting go. Then I tried an exercise I call my "Garage Sale."

I made a list of all the "stuff" I was "holding on to," that I wanted to let go, then I "priced" it. How much would it cost? What could I do? What needed to be said and to whom, before I could let it go? I spent about a week doing this, then one Saturday I had my personal "garage sale".

I tried to get rid of everything I had on my list in one day. I made a lot of telephone calls, and several visits. Sure, I tried to get my asking price, but sometimes I had to negotiate. I always managed to hear the other side of the story that I was too narrow-minded to understand before. That in itself was a wonderful lesson.

The "garage sale" makes letting go an event. I have time to prepare for the release. Once it's sold, it's gone.

68. FANTASY

As a kid, I often fantasized that I'd been adopted, and some day my real mom and dad would come and take me away. I spent most of my time daydreaming, reading books, watching TV, and going to movies—anything to avoid facing the realities of my life.

As an adult, I used my fantasies to avoid my feelings, and keep me trapped in a job I hated and a marriage that was emotionally damaging. I lived in the future, not the now. Things were always going to get better someday. I dreamed about traveling, about how I would spend the money from my next promotion, about buying a new car "next year."

In recovery, I began to see how I was burying my present feelings behind the daydreams. I started keeping a journal, and now when I feel myself drifting back into dreams, I write down how I feel at this moment. With the encouragement of my group, I've found a new job that is challenging and fulfilling. My relationships are improving with openness and honesty. I am learning to trust my feelings and myself. I am getting to know the real me.

69. INVENTORY

I feared Step Four. It has quite a reputation. But I applied the "Keep It Simple" principle and with a tablet in hand I drew the simple outline from pages 65 and 66 in the Big Book. Then I dug out my dictionary to define "searching," "fearless," "moral," and "inventory."

"Searching" I easily connected to an Easter egg hunt: under everything, and in all the usual and unexpected places. "Fearless" also was easy for me to visualize: God was either everything or nothing, and my choice had been made in Step Three. I did have some anxiety, but I really felt I was on a do-or-die mission. "Inventory" was the easiest for me: a list is just that, itemized, tabulated, and accounted for. But "moral" presented me with a problem.

I finally realized it was not a good/bad issue. There was no judgment involved, but to me "moral" implied just that. The dictionary says "moral" means dealing with right or wrong behavior. "Wrong" meant "*not in accordance with justice*." "Accordance" meant "*harmony, agreement*." "Right" meant "*cor-*

rect or in accordance with fact." These definitions helped me understand that my list of behaviors was a vehicle for me to see what I was doing that worked, and what I was doing that didn't work.

My fear about some of my actions, my embarrassment, and my shame were related to my old thinking that I was a bad person. The Fourth Step is not about being bad. It is about gaining clarity about what I wanted to have as part of my life. Before I could change, before I could accept responsibility for recovery, set boundaries, and lead a full life, I had to know more about me. This was the Step, the work, the exercise at hand.

70. WRONG IS NOT THE SAME AS BAD

Growing up, various people told me I was bad when I made mistakes. I believed them. No matter what I did, it was wrong and I was bad. Now that I work the Steps, I see that I have always had the tools to be a whole person. I had just been using them for the wrong jobs, like using the handle of a screwdriver to pound a nail instead of a hammer. It works pretty good, but it is not the appropriate tool for the job.

I grew up in a family that used the wrong tools. We used guilt and shame most often, and we used them to manipulate each other, for control. As a child,

I felt guilt and shame, as if I were bad, when really, I was just wrong. I was human. I made mistakes.

Being wrong is a learning experience. When I allow myself or others to be wrong, I create the space for learning and for experiencing freedom. When anyone (including myself) makes a mistake it is an opportunity, and for that I am grateful.

71. HIGHER POWER

God *as I understood God* meant one-third guardian angel, one-third the Force, and one-third flower child (the sixties variety).

I also learned from the AA Big Book that it had to be a loving God. A friend suggested I tell myself, "God is with me, all is well, and I am grateful" (because God likes to hear thank you). So this is how I envisioned the Power that was going to restore me to sanity. This Power would never reach in and lift me out of a storm, but it would reach down and take my hand whenever I invited it to, and it would give me the courage and skill to walk free in the world. To begin with, I just had to be willing to believe. As I practiced believing, and kept working the Steps, I would come to believe.

Like building muscles for a flat belly, I work at this every day; spiritual muscles depend on my daily relationship with my HP. I practice, and I read my daily thoughts book. I picture in my mind's eye a cloud of loving energy like the Force, following me around like a guardian angel, saying Peace & Love. I ask the Force to love me, guide me, and protect me. I thank it, and I do what is in front of me to do. After a few weeks, I realized I was coming to believe.

72. GRATITUDE

When I was just over a year in recovery, I took a bus trip from Chicago to Phoenix, Arizona. It wasn't planned; I'd been on a cross-country trip, had a fight with my companion, and I was stuck. "A victim again," my old thinking said. Wouldn't you know, there was a screaming baby and an inept mother on board. They undoubtedly were on board as part of a cosmic conspiracy to harass me.

As I looked around for validation of my suffering, I caught the eye of a woman about my age, sitting two rows behind me. The baby wailed and I rolled my eyes, shook my head, and pointed toward the front of the bus. She looked away, but in a few minutes she handed me a note. "I am deaf. What did you say?" I was speechless. She smiled at me, and pointed at the paper for me to write on as if to clear my confusion.

"Hi," I wrote. "My name is Joan. Where are you traveling to?"

I don't remember if the baby cried anymore or not. I do remember the welling up of love and gratitude I had. Once again, in spite of myself, I knew that my Higher Power was doing for me what I couldn't do for myself.

73. STARFISH

Early one morning I was walking down the beach as the tide was going out. I saw a man coming the other way. I noticed as he approached that he would occasionally stop, pick up a starfish stranded by the outgoing tide, look at it, then throw the starfish out into the sea.

When we met, I asked him what he was doing.

"Well, if the starfish are still on the sand when the sun comes up and hits them, they will surely die. I merely throw them back in the sea and give them a chance to live."

I responded: "But there are hundreds of miles of beach and you are just one man. Does what you are doing really matter?"

He picked up another starfish, looked at it, and threw it out into the sea. "It does to that one," he said.

I think this little story fits all of us in recovery. Aren't we all starfish on the beach? I know that I was and someone threw me back into the sea of life for one more chance. It matters to me, so now I walk the beach when the tide's going out, in search of starfish.

74. SUGAR MAMA

I might as well have had an illuminated sign atop my car and a neon sign in the front window of my home—"CODEPENDENT WILL HIRE."

For years, seemingly any good-looking male applicant could have the cushy job of filling the void in my life that I referred to as my "empty arm." I was particularly attracted to men who "needed" me for what I could offer, and what I could offer was money.

I am a daughter of the first generation of "I Am Woman, Hear Me Roar" mothers. When I turned thirteen and boys began to ask me out on dates, my parents told me the same thing over and over again. "Here's some money. Don't wait for him to pay for everything. Remember, you don't owe him anything." Consequently, I was petrified that if a boy asked me out and paid for *anything*, I would owe him a roll in the hay. So it became a habit for me to pay for virtually everything.

Despite my mother's influence, June Cleaver's dialogues in "Leave It To Beaver," and Cybil Shepard's Cover Girl commercials led me to believe that a woman without a man was nobody. So even if I had to buy him, I wanted a man on my arm to prove I was *somebody*.

As the years rolled by, I was comfortable with nothing less than picking up the entire tab any time I was out with a man. I collected a lot of head garbage along the way, like "men can't be trusted, men are motivated only by sex," etc., etc. In order to feel *safe* and *in control*, I had to pay for everything. I rationalized this inequity by telling myself that any physical advances or commitments that occurred were then on *my* terms—which of course, was okay.

Like every good codependent, I soon took on caretaking of these adorable men. I "won them over" with great dinners, doing their laundry to their specifications, and creating expensive getaways for the two of us. I would give them anything money could buy within my credit limit, and that credit limit was all that ever stopped me. I paid for all kinds of adventures from skydiving to weekends in Tahiti. I was a real Sugar Mama.

Naturally, these men enjoyed my "generosity," and each of them would stay with me for awhile, but my confidence in my personality, intellect, and appearance was little to none. This Sugar Mama routine was a way of keeping a string attached to them without necessarily demanding a commitment.

We practiced "open communication" so that we could freely express ourselves to each other. I rewarded them simply for being honest. "I can handle anything as long as it is the truth," I would say. Sometimes their honesty was brutal. They would tell me that they were sleeping with other women or seeing someone else. I would be crushed inside, but all I could muster up to say would be, "Thanks for being honest with me." I couldn't bring myself to "punish" them by ending the relationship, because, after all, they had been truthful. This was the pattern that was pathetically consistent in each of my relationships. I couldn't understand *why* this kept happening to me.

One particular man that I was involved with, "John," came to tell me that despite my monogamy to him, he was routinely sleeping with two other women. John told me how thankful he was that I was so understanding, so that he could get this off his chest. He said he finally felt satisfied in his needs because each of us contributed an even third to his fulfillment! I was devastated.

Something inside me began to boil. I became disgusted with myself and John. I realized that my self-esteem and self-worth had hit rock bottom. At that point, I couldn't imagine feeling any lower. I broke up with John ruthlessly. Any bridges that may have been left available I burned, so that I could not turn back.

It was amazing how much better I felt without John—and all of the other "Johns" before him. It had been such a simple solution, and I wasn't alone or lonely as I had feared. Within a few weeks I dated more than I ever had before. I dated men who were attracted to me for who I was, rather than what material luxuries I could afford to give them. Relationships have been healthier for me since then.

75. ACCEPTANCE

"I'll show you what acceptance is." That was my angry, self-willed, determined attitude. Then, in recovery, I learned that acceptance was not an attitude but a way of life. I didn't know how to do anything, except to get an attitude, get fired up, and get it done.

I learned that to live in acceptance required my taking action to change me in three areas: physical, spiritual, and emotional/mental. One day at a time, I must keep taking action if I wanted to keep experiencing acceptance (the key to freedom from codependency and living life on life's terms).

The physical solution for me is willingness: "I will," instead of "I won't." I am a fist-maker; when anyone tells me to change, I make a fist with my hand and my mind. So for one week, I tried to open my palms and be willing, like getting ready to catch a ball. I had to wait until someone pitched to me. I couldn't tell anyone when to throw, just be ready if they did.

The second week, I practiced thinking differently. I chose to focus my thoughts on the idea that I extend my open hands to an open mind. I practiced by saying "the world might not be flat." It helped me not take myself so seriously. With my hands open, and my mind open, and my sense of humor at least in the same room, I began to practice honesty and humility to bridge the mental/emotional to the spiritual.

By being willing enough to be open-minded enough to admit that this new way worked for thousands and it might work for me, too, I admitted that the way I had been living wasn't working. This honesty, combined with willingness and open-mindedness, gave me a chance to experience humility.

Humility included me saying, "I don't know, I don't have to know, and it is O.K. not to know." I was willing to receive an answer, a suggestion to find an answer, or that there was not an answer yet, from whatever source my HP chose. At this point, I experienced and felt acceptance.

76. CONTROL

When I was growing up, everything was either good or bad, right or wrong. When I misbehaved, my parents took away privileges and withdrew affection. I still shudder when I remember my father's icy stares of disapproval.

When I started my own family, I was still carrying around the attitude I learned from my parents. I was a complainer, always finding fault with everyone around me. I was full of advice on how my children, my husband, my co-workers should behave. I was self-righteous and judgmental.

Through my codependency recovery group, I began to gain insight into why I acted this way. Because my parents punished any sign of weakness—anger, fear, jealousy, uncertainty—I had learned to conceal those feelings behind being "right." I denied that I ever felt that way, and that others around me felt those emotions, too.

In recovery, I work on giving up blame and guilt-tripping. I've begun to take responsibility for my own feelings instead of managing the feelings of others. I admitted that I had been trying to manipulate and control them, and hardest of all, I admitted that I sometimes felt the same feelings I disliked in others.

As I've let go my need to manipulate and control, I have begun to feel less stressed, and to complain less. With honest communication, the people around me are more cooperative and friendly. Recovery has expanded my relationships, and given me freedom to work on taking care of myself.

77. NUMB

Gloria enjoyed being busy. She worked a full-time job, utilizing her vocational school skills. She exercised aerobically three times a week for an hour and a half, because her husband liked her to keep fit. She was active in the PTA, and took her kids to music and dance lessons three times per week since those classes had been dropped off the curriculum when the school levy failed. Gloria was an immaculate housekeeper and did all her family's laundry and ironing. She just couldn't see why they should spend good money paying someone else to do it when she preferred her own methods anyway. Gloria remembered to floss her teeth every day. She made three meals a day, every day, including brown-bag lunches for her kids and her husband during the week.

Gloria was quite a gardener, too. She cultivated all types of exotic herbs and vegetables. She learned to use them in all sorts of gourmet recipes. She entertained regularly, and enjoyed hostessing dinner parties for her husband's clients. She gave five hours a week and five percent of her income to charity, whether or not she felt she could afford it. "Give until it hurts, and then give a little more" prevailed as the theme of Gloria's life.

One day during aerobics class, Gloria twisted her left ankle and fell down. A classmate helped her up, and she assured him she was okay. She felt no pain, so she completed the class.

Two days later, after another aerobics class, Gloria noticed she couldn't put on her left street shoe. To her surprise, her ankle had swollen considerably, but it still didn't hurt. So she wrapped it in a gauze bandage and put on a boot instead. She was on her way to visit a friend in the hospital who had just had a baby. As she exited the elevator on the maternity ward, she collapsed. Nurses rushed to her side and they took her to the emergency room.

The doctors told Gloria she had shattered her ankle during the aerobics class two days previous.

They told her that her inability to feel pain was common in people who maintained a schedule such as Gloria's, without taking time for herself. Over the years, her mind had learned to block out pain signals that her nervous system was desperately trying to send to her mind. For many years, Gloria's life revolved around others, rather than herself. She focused on how *they* appeared to other people. She did this because she was unhappy with herself, lacking self-esteem, and self-responsibility. She was in pain, but could never feel it, because she never paid any attention to herself.

Her doctor recommended that she join CoDA. Now Gloria regularly attends meetings and focuses her Twelve Step work on balancing her personal needs and her family responsibilities.

78. MY GARDEN

I've been able to relate my recovery to a garden of beautiful flowers. Someone had planted the seeds, but it was up to me to surrender and begin the growing process (Step 1). In this garden, I can see the beauty of the love, compassion, caring, and sharing with others.

The sun shines down with warmth to help me and my garden grow. I see this as my Higher Power (God) and love from my fellow members and my sponsor. Then the clouds roll in—this is my pain and sorrow, and from this rain (tears) and the storms of life, my garden and I grow and flourish. After the storms pass, the sun sparkles on the raindrops, and I know each time my H.P. is *always* there for me. In this I can find trust (Steps 2 and 3). My flowers cannot grow without a little fertilizer—*never* too much, because then my flowers would burn up and die. Such would be my recovery.

Then there are weeds I need to keep clearing away by doing the 4th and 5th Steps. And by doing the 10th Step daily I can try to keep the weeds of life from choking my beautiful flowers. The tools of the Program help me, for without them I would have no suggested way to keep my garden in order.

The large weeds that are stubborn and hard to get rid of I keep plugging away at "one day at a time" with Steps 6 and 7. These are my defects of character. I try to make amends without becoming self-righteous. This is all part of my growing process (Steps 8 and 9). Prayer and meditation help nurture my garden every day (Step 11).

Then with time there come small seeds that are carried on the wind (voice and example) of my experience, strength, and hope of a better way of life to those who are suffering, in and out of recovery (Step 12).

Then perhaps another garden can grow and find the beauty, peace, and serenity that the Fellowship promises if I am willing to practice these principles.

But if I choose to relapse, my garden becomes as if a *nuclear bomb* had struck, barren and with no life, for then I am lost.

79. WHY I HAD TO QUIT RETAIL

As an assistant buyer for a large department store, I frequently worked a six-day week, and seven days between Thanksgiving and January 31. I dressed like they do in the latest issue of *Vogue* with my hair coiffed and makeup perfectly applied. I never requested reimbursement for mileage or parking for checking on suburban stores or executive errands. I never turned down an assignment no matter how loaded my schedule was—if that meant skipping all meals and cancelling personal plans, then so be it. The rules were: never say "no"; never ask for a raise, even though we literally made less than welfare mothers did; be tough with vendors and subordinates, and a marshmallow with supervisors; never share your displeasure with anyone, or any situation that comes your way, because you are going to be in the position you are in until it is convenient for "Them" to promote you, or until you were fired.

I got caught up in the glamour of the job. I worked with people who went to Manhattan every month. I saw the new fashions before the press did. I helped compose advertisements that would be in the newspaper. I had an eye for color, fabric, design, and hanger-appeal, or so my supervisors told me. Basically, I played with clothes all day and I found that very exciting.

Of course, the flip side to this was that upper management saw that I was continually more productive, the more they pushed me. I relocated several times to take a new position at their request. I would do anything they asked. Their moods swung like a pendulum, which just added coal to the fire of excitement. What a "value" I was! (What a *sucker* I was!) They continued to pile on the work, and I would dutifully plow through it all, manicuring every detail. I was twenty-two years old. I lived on my own. I had no personal life. I began to get backaches. I picked up every strain of flu that came through. I didn't sleep well. I attributed all of these conditions to my "hard work," that I took very seriously. I felt a certain type of ownership for my responsibilities, and they became my family.

I told myself I enjoyed working hard. My parents approved of my working so many hours because it demonstrated to them and the world that I was a hard worker, a true virtue in my family, and it was important to me to please my parents. After all, they raised me and paid for my lifetime meal ticket, college. I felt I owed them the pleasure of seeing me succeed. Working hard was the way to succeed, so that's what I sought to do. I *was* my job.

My anxiety level got so high that I couldn't eat anymore. I fainted several times on the job. As I lay down in the sick room after a fainting spell, Personnel suggested that I use some of my vacation time. I had a month of vacation coming, and if I didn't use it, I would lose it. I took a month off to enjoy the outdoors and visit my family. After two weeks had passed, I finally began to relax. I began to realize that I was *really sick*. I realized I was sick in my thinking. I needed a healthier environment. After my vacation was over, I quit my buying career.

I had heard about Co-Dependents Anonymous, and out of desperation and emptiness I went to my first meeting. I listened to the others tell their stories, which were *my* stories. Even in that very first meeting, I discovered that other people had lived a similar lifestyle and wanted to change. I learned that the system I was in was not the only way to live. I learned that I could change my habits by confronting my fears and anxieties through the Twelve Steps. Since then, I work my Steps regularly. I have become a much healthier and happier person.

80. TEACHABLE

Shoulds and shouldn'ts determined how I acted. The number one item on the list was *you* should. *You*, not me, should be teachable, should change, should whatever, and I would naturally be different. Someone in a meeting gave me a list of the "principles," but I had no clue how I should handle these. I quite honestly thought I was doing a rather good job with most of them, especially humility and willingness. The problem as I saw it was that I was *too* humble and willing, and that was what made me codependent. After sharing my perspective at a meeting, and evoking a few laughs, I asked my sponsor for help. I wanted to tell her how to convince the others that I was right. She asked me to be willing to think differently. I felt defensive immediately. I was at her house, wasn't I? I was willing to ask her, wasn't I?

We stopped and she asked me tell her what feelings I had that made me come to CoDA. Identifying feelings other than "good" and "bad" took work for me. Then she wanted me to say what feelings I had when we started working together. That was easy: pain and fear. Next she said, "What feelings do you have as you stop and breathe and practice the new way?" By this time, I felt anxious and threatened. "You experience pain," she told me, "until you are willing to be different. Being teachable is when you have tried everything you know how and then are willing to stop doing and start being."

I knew in my head that I was dying living the old way, and that I was willing to try everything I was told to do, but I just couldn't get a handle on things. I memorized the words, took a job washing ashtrays, hunted down newcomers, and shared my phone number, but somewhere I missed whatever it was that allowed laughter and jokes. Nothing was funny to me. My heart was breaking and it seemed that no one cared.

Through my despair, a member pointed out that I had learned to keep coming back, no matter what, and to keep working, no matter what. I asked, "Then why do I feel so bad?" I was told that in order to learn and grow, a student had to be ready. Just like a field that needs to be fertilized, watered, seeded, weeded, and nurtured, so too, we need to prepare to receive recovery. At this point, I knew that I had learned. I felt different and good and glad. Even though I had not understood why, I had been willing and I had learned. I was teachable.

81. SEDUCTION OF GRATIFICATION

Attractive packages seem to give me freedom, but they don't. When I feed the anxiety of my powerlessness with doubt and fear, the sense of need that I experience demands satisfaction. I feel as if I have to have something or someone *now*. The Big Book says, "We had to have a power by which we could live." It means a Higher Power. My head says use whatever is handy.

When I quit drinking and doing drugs I knew that "lack of power was our dilemma" referred to the chemical fuel that gave me power, and I truly believed that God was my only Power. Then around six years into recovery, I found that void of emptiness one more time in my guts.

My head told me, no problem, go to a meeting, get a newcomer. But my experience was that no matter how many newcomers I sponsored, no matter how many times I worked the Steps, I still felt the void. So I went to my own sponsor, who took me through the Steps one more time.

Working Step Two together, I made a list of all the things that gave me satisfaction when I was frustrated. With, "What do I do to feel OK?" at the top of the page, we began. My sponsor reminded me that this was not about being good or bad, just about what I was doing that worked or didn't work. I found that my *sanity savers* included rescuing sponsees, their sponsees, neighbors, friends, strangers in parking lots. In fact, anyone who might need a third hand got one of mine, like it or not. I got caught up in others' lives. It was such a noble way to avoid mine. I knew exactly how each person felt, and what they should do, but I had lost track of me. Repeating the same actions and expecting different results was the insanity. I expected powers to restore me to sanity that weren't big enough for the job. In fact, I kept me crazy by doing this.

My sponsor and I discussed this list. I found that I was really attached to each one. They were my most intimate friends and commitments. I had rationalized using the Twelfth Step into using others to avoid me, and it was killing me. I did have to have a power by which I could live, but none of these was big enough.

I even used "feeling feelings" as a power. Nothing like a good rage, a case of lust (for shopping or men), or a bout of self-pity to feel justified and powerful. But even the feelings I used weren't big enough. My sponsor helped me see how I continued to experience insanity by thinking "This time it will be different." We saw that these powers *seemed* to work, they all gave me immediate gratification, but they never restored me to sanity. "If only, as soon as, this time it'll be different"—these thoughts had to be exchanged for patterns that worked.

This was the beginning of a process to find and follow a Higher Power that could restore me to sanity. I couldn't know all of my HP at once. All I could be sure of was that it was of my own choosing, and that it was a loving, benevolent Power. I needed to be willing to view my HP from several angles. HP would never be limited to three dimensions, and therefore would appear different at different times, but my HP would always be mine.

82. ANGER

Yeah, I was angry. I was afraid sometimes. I was lonely too. Wouldn't you be if you had my life? It was full, and I was busy. "Let's take care of each other" didn't work for me any longer, though, and that is when I finally came to CoDA.

By working the Steps, I could see that my walls had blinded me to who I was and what I was feeling.

I was focusing on others and not myself. With my new focus of "How do I feel?" I can set a boundary. I can be responsible for me. I can talk about me and the pain I feel. Skipping the "I feel..." part seemed so natural for me. It never occurred to me that this was the set-up for my codependency and my denial of myself in order to avoid looking at me. I began to understand that I had forgotten how to walk in my own shoes. I knew instantly why I hated the expression, "Get a Life." It was because I didn't have one.

I have an incredible talent, developed over many years, of acutely analyzing *you*, summing *you* up, and telling *you* what you need to do to take care of you. The scary part is not that I am accurate, but how much I enjoy doing it, and how often I do it. The worst part is that this creates terrible resentments in you because I do for you what you (and only you) can do for yourself. You back away from me. I become more and more alone. The sick part is that this is the very basis of my codependency. As I stay so wrapped up in you, I can never have time for me.

Stopping the almost automatic rhythm of looking at you instead of me takes practice. In the beginning I carried a 3x5 card that said, "When you do _____, I feel _____." This helped me know what felt good or bad so I could begin to choose what I wanted in my life. I kept a list. I was surprised how many times I let things in my life when I didn't like them or want them. I just didn't know how to say no.

Getting me to feel feelings made me mad. It is funny now, but I had spent so much of my life carefully concealing any indication of my feelings, that I felt terribly threatened by myself when I started to feel. To help, a fellow member took me on practice runs. We went to every sad, funny, scary movie around. We listened to the blues at three in the morning and got depressed together. We went to Disneyland and screamed our way through the rides. We kept lists of each new feeling we could identify. We did it together and felt together, and we did it for ourselves. I learned to walk beside her, not for her. I learned to feel my feelings and let her feel hers. I learned freedom.

83. REALITY

Learning to experience my own reality, who I really was, meant I had to pay attention to my feelings, my thoughts, and my actions. It meant I had to stop relying on others' feedback to be me.

This process was painful. I feared my Fourth Step inventory because I was afraid to find out how awful

I was. Worse, I feared finding out how awful my life had been. I didn't want to go back and acknowledge my painful years as a child. I hated thinking about it, much less writing about it and sharing it with another.

Listening in a Step meeting, I learned that others felt the same way. I also learned that whether or not I acknowledged my past, it was coloring my present and my future, and would continue to do so until I learned to own all of who I was. Only then could I create the person I was intended to be by my loving Higher Power. The options took some thinking. On the one hand, I knew I was miserable and had been for years, but the fear of change fed my sick thinking. Immediately I thought, "But was it really that bad?" *YES, IT WAS.*

A lot of the pain of my life turned out to be fear. Feeling the pain of the actual behaviors and patterns was less than the magnified version I relived in my mind. The hidden secrets I had repressed, denied, avoided, and minimized were less painful as I brought them out into the light. Knowing I had begun a process by using the Steps, I had hope for the first time. The freedom from the chains of my past, plus the hope of freedom in the future, and the trust I had learned to develop in my Higher Power gave me courage.

84. PAYING ATTENTION TO THE PAIN

One tool I used when I began recovery was the joy in the eyes of those I heard sharing in meetings. I hadn't experienced that yet, but I knew when they talked about their pain, I felt something inside that words didn't touch. I felt those same kind of indescribable feelings when they spoke of joy, too.

From my new-found friends, I learned the only way to have joy in my life was to pay attention to the pain. As paradoxical as it sounded at first, I have learned that this is true. The walls I had always used to block pain had also blocked joy. As I remove the walls, I can begin to form boundaries instead. Boundaries protect me from pain, but they do not block out joy like walls do. I still feel pain with my new-found boundaries, but instead of ignoring it, I pay attention. I believe that pain is a tool I can use to adjust my boundaries. I'm not so afraid of it now. It gives me an opportunity to be real, and the nicest part of this new reality is that it includes joy. My heart can sing again.

85. AM I BEING HONEST?

We've heard around the tables that this is an honest Program. And it is! Before coming into the Program we were liars, cheaters, and generally all-around dishonest, especially with ourselves. Then we began recovery, found out that it is an honest Program, found out that it was time to start getting honest, and started to grow when we got honest with ourselves, our Higher Power, and other people.

It's been said that in order to get honest with others, we must get honest with ourselves first. How are we going to be honest with others or with ourselves? Tough question, isn't it? We learn it one day at a time—just like everything else. If we want this Program to work for us, honesty plays a big part in our recovery and we cannot "skip over it."

A big part of honesty is being honest about the Program, knowing that we can't work it on our own because our way didn't work. We need the help of sponsors and the Twelve Steps, and most of all we need our Higher Power. All we have to do is reach out and ask, and that unconditional love the Fellowship has will be there for us. But nobody can reach out for us; we have to do it ourselves!

Steps Four and Five help us get a lot of honesty. That's when we get rid of all the garbage (if we're honest) and clean house, so to speak. There's no such thing as "perfect honesty." The best we can do is to work and strive for a better way or quality of honesty.

Honesty with ourselves and others will help us stay and grow. So let's stop and ask ourselves, "Am I being honest with myself and others?"

86. STRESSED OUT

I was a stress junkie for years. As supervisor of an extremely busy word processing center, I had a lot of responsibility, but no control over the demands made on my department. I felt overworked and underpaid, always running to keep up with deadlines and make up for other people's mistakes. I had no time for myself or my family. I took work home with me on weekends, and spent all my time on my home computer. I had headaches all the time.

I went to stress management classes. I took an aerobics class. I drank a lot of coffee and chain-smoked cigarettes to "relax" me. I got more and more harried and resentful.

Then my back went out, and I was forced to take time off work and stop my exercise classes. I was in despair. I thought I would never catch up with all the work that needed to be done, but I was helpless to do anything about it. It was a shock when I realized the company was managing to get along without me. The classes I had taken had encouraged me to believe that, if I learned enough techniques, I could do it all. My body was clearly telling me I couldn't.

I had read about codependency, and suspected that I might be one. During my time away from work, I started attending meetings of a codependency recovery group. When I went back to my job, I began to find ways to reduce the stress I felt. I quit assuming all the responsibility for results and stopped covering up other people's mistakes. I began setting aside time just to relax and enjoy myself.

With the self-knowledge I'm gaining through recovery, I am learning to let go of the idea that I can control anything or anyone besides myself. I'm working on getting rid of denial and getting to know my true feelings, needs, and wants. I'm letting go and letting God take over.

87. LETTING GO IS NOT ENOUGH

"You cannot take the directions out of context, and letting go is only half of it." The speaker said that if you let go without letting God, you are skipping Steps Two and Three. You might let go and let the Dodgers, or the Pistons, or a new car or HIM. No, he said, not God-HIM, but the good-looking guy HIM. Or HER, never confused with God by the men.

("Her" is that spiritual wonder that the boys talk about when they find a higher power other than God.)

When I let go without a Higher Power, I leave myself without a power in my life. Almost like a law of gravity, affirming "I am powerless" without inviting my Higher Power in right behind, is dangerous. I acknowledge the void, identify what I am powerless over, all the unmanageability, but then I must use my will to ask God for His will.

I tried all sorts of powers to restore me to balance and sanity. I let go over and over and let whatever was there fill the void. It never dawned on me that I could choose what power I wanted to let in my life. As I worked and re-worked my Steps, I included cars and credit cards and shopping and whatever on my lists of *sanity savers*. I'd let go and do it different, or get a new hairdo, but each time, the solution was let go AND LET GOD. I sit in awe now at the tremendous power that my God holds in my life. He so gently teaches me to let Him guide me. The same old surrender is the answer: Let Go, and Let God.

88. IS CODEPENDENCY A DISEASE?

The argument at coffee lasted past our normal one-hour social gathering. The discussion was started by a recovering alcoholic who had begun attending

CoDA meetings. He insisted that alcoholism was a disease, but questioned that codependency was. Are we ever cured?

The group came to no black and white answers. We all agreed, however, that whatever codependency was, it had been slowly killing each of us, and its deadly effects influenced all we came in contact with. We also all agreed that although there may be other solutions to alleviate codependency, we had chosen this one, and in order to find recovery, we were going to meetings and following directions.

When I got home, I pulled out my dictionary. "Disease" is defined as *any departure from health; illness in general; or a particular disorder with a specific cause and characteristic symptoms.* Codependency certainly was a disease in my understanding: predictable symptoms, lack of balance, and for me, the idea of departure from health reminded me of the Second Step, "restored to sanity." We had it, but somewhere we had departed from it.

The next week at coffee, I brought up my findings. I believe that when I live in the symptoms of codependency, I have a disease. When I am living in the solution, I have a condition of codependency, but it is not an active disease. This condition must be treated on a daily basis, in a spiritual manner, in order to remain arrested. I am recovered in the sense that my condition is not active, but not cured. If I do not practice my recovery on a daily basis, I lose it, and I still have the disease.

89. NICE

I grew up in a compulsively "nice" family. Everyone was very polite. No one ever shouted or raised their voices. When my parents were angry, they simply withdrew and denied that anything was wrong. Feelings were not important; niceness was.

Neither of my folks was ever there for me. If I had a problem, my parents' reaction was to bury and deny it. After awhile, I quit trying to connect with them, and just pretended that I had no feelings.

Before I got into recovery, I was involved in several relationships that ended when my girlfriends accused me of being too cold. I was afraid of showing any emotions. I froze at the slightest sign of conflict. Most of the time, I drifted, just letting things happen to me, and doing whatever seemed easiest.

I was like a rudderless ship, unable to identify my own values and needs. Without feelings, I couldn't get feedback from other people about my perceptions of situations and behaviors.

With the encouragement of my group, I started trying to get in touch with how I felt. I made a list of words that described feelings such as angry, afraid, excited, sad, happy. I carried the list in my wallet, and used it to help me name my feelings. I kept an inventory of my encounters with others, and used that to study how I felt. I began to experience life more richly and deeply than ever before. I'm learning to live, instead of just existing. I'm no longer out of touch.

90. FOR TODAY ONLY

There are two days in every week about which we should not worry, two days which should be kept from fear and apprehension.

One of these days is **Yesterday**, with its mistakes and cares, its faults and blunders, its aches and pains. Yesterday has passed forever beyond our control.

All the money in the world cannot bring back yesterday. We cannot undo a single act we performed; we cannot erase a single word we said. Yesterday is gone.

The other day we should not worry about is **Tomorrow**, with its possible adversaries, its burdens, its large promise and poor performance. Tomorrow is beyond our immediate control. Tomorrow's sun will rise. Until it does, we have no stake in tomorrow, for it is yet unborn.

This leaves only one day: **Today**. Anyone can fight the battles of just one day. It is only when you and I add the burdens of those two awful eternities— yesterday and tomorrow—that we break down.

It is not the experience of today that drives people crazy. It is resentment or bitterness for something which happened yesterday, and the fear of what tomorrow may bring. Let us, therefore, live but *one day at a time*.

91. INSIDE JOB

I sat in the doctor's office, having my eyes examined. He slipped disk after disk in the machine, asking, "Is this better or worse?" As I responded, I realized he was believing me. He was actually relying on my responses. He was relying on *me*. I almost cried. I couldn't remember anyone else, including me, ever really believing what I had said. Someone was actually honoring my reality.

My thoughts flashed back to shoe stores. When I was a child, my mother had argued with shoe salesmen that her daughter's feet were not that big. I thought of how my little toes curl under to this day. I thought of my family's various comments on how I dressed. I had always trusted their judgment, but as the words crossed my mind's eye, I realized that what I had really done was deny my own judgment to dress in a way that pleased them, no matter what I thought I looked like.

My mother loved sailor dresses. My short, square body looked like a potato in those dresses, but it sure put a twinkle in my mother's eye. I thought that meant she loved me.

My heart ached to be loved, and as I thought about my pain, I remembered what I had heard at a meeting. A woman had said, "I am very needy. What I need the most is me." I thought about her, and about myself, and knew I needed to be loved, to begin knowing who I am, to begin loving who I am.

For so many years I had thought it came from my family or some other outside source. Now I knew that for me reality was indeed an "inside job."

92. THE TRUTH OF WHO I AM

I stood in front of my mirror one more time, trying to decide if I was fat. I knew the numbers on the bathroom scale, but I honestly could not "see" me. An old boyfriend had told me I looked really skinny in a certain pair of jeans. I pulled them on, but still couldn't tell. I had no sense of my physical reality, and I didn't know what to think about it. For years, I hadn't really looked at myself in the mirror. Oh, I saw that hems were even, colors matched, the outside looked acceptable, but I had no idea what I really looked like.

My best friend "dressed" me for parties and job interviews. I sought her input when I bought new glasses or tried a new hairstyle. My only perception of how I looked was what she or others said about my appearance. This state of being was normal to me, so when I started my recovery I was amazed to hear that a common characteristic of codependency was an inability to experience one's own reality. This made me kind of panicky. It was one more sign of just how codependent I was and how powerless and crazy I felt. Not only did I not know what my reality was, I had no idea how to begin to experience it. My reality, as I knew it, was *your* reality, no matter who you were.

In a meeting, I heard a woman say that she had to learn all over again to use her senses. Starting with her feet, she practiced feeling the ground under her shoes. She paid attention to surfaces: rough, hard, carpeted, soft, hot or cold. She also paid attention to what her feet felt like inside her shoes. Were her toes being cramped? Were her heels rubbing? Were there wrinkles in her socks? Were her feet too warm, too sweaty, or too cold? Everyone in the meeting laughed with her as she talked about her feet. She held them up and carried on a conversation with them.

She said that by learning first to "listen" to her feet, she also learned to listen to her head and her heart. She learned to pay attention to what *she* wanted for herself, instead of determining her wants by what pleased others. She began by listening to her thoughts and then honoring them by following through with the appropriate action. "Yes, Mr. Toe," she would say, "You say you're being pinched? Well then, let's just put you in a different shoe. How's that?" We all laughed, but I began to think, too.

"You like that? Are you a happy toe? Are the rest of my toes happy?" As she sat pretending to listen to her toes, I started listening to me. First, I was awed that I really got to choose for myself. Then I went from toes to head checking my comfort level. I didn't like the jeans I was wearing. They weren't comfortable. I thought, "It doesn't matter if I am skinny or fat. I am me. The truth is I am a person, and I want to know this person. I want to know what makes me happy and sad and what makes me who I am."

I have listened to everyone else's heads and hearts my whole life. Now I am learning to listen to me.

93. DENIAL

I had been in the Codependents Anonymous Program for five years. I was doing one more Fourth and Fifth Step. My sponsor stopped me, and commented that she had heard the same relationship issues before. Although I loved and trusted this woman, I felt defensive at once. I read to her what I had written this time about the relationships in my life. After cutting away all my description, it said, "It is not my fault. I have no blame in this situation. I am right. I am a victim. Poor me." That's how I felt, too.

I had not only continued to volunteer to be victimized, but by doing so, I was able to keep my role as victim. I wouldn't have to change. I wouldn't have to practice the principle of responsibility. I wouldn't have to set boundaries. I wouldn't have to risk people not liking me.

I discovered that suffering was one of my most intimate "friends." I was dependent on people in my life to give me suffering. It was predictable from them and I perpetuated it. Suffering supported the self-image that kept me sick. It seemed so real. It seemed like it wasn't my fault. It seemed like it was the only way I could live, but I knew better. I had invited suffering into my life and enabled people to victimize me in a deadly, fear-filled attempt to avoid being me.

Long before I had ever done drugs or drank, my pattern showed that I was a victim. Just like a spider, I lured people into my web, used them to hurt me, then blamed them for it and found my next catch. It was such a powerful role. I was terrified. I felt like a newcomer, naked and vulnerable.

Victims are powerful volunteers. My denial was a protection that my Higher Power had allowed me to keep until I was ready to change. I felt scared, but hopeful. Nothing is revealed to me before I am ready to look at it. Denial is not about being good or bad.

94. RISKS

I always liked living on the edge. I was the black sheep of my family, always trying to shock or impress them with the outrageous things I said and did. I liked taking risks. I took flying lessons and got my pilot's license so I could learn aerobatics—I didn't want to fly straight and level, I wanted to be upside down or sideways. I drank and did drugs for the same reasons. I was busy all the time.

Then two weeks before my wedding, my fiance abruptly cancelled our marriage. He told me he liked being wild and crazy sometimes, but he couldn't keep up with my constant quest for new thrills.

My loneliness and depression finally got me into recovery. I joined AA and gave up alcohol and drugs. Gradually, I began to get glimpses of the reasons for my thrill-seeking. I had used substances to help me feel like part of a group, so I didn't have to be lonely. I kept busy to keep from feeling depressed. My constant search for excitement kept me from being aware of my pain. A friend suggested I go to a CoDA meeting. I did, and learned a lot about why I was a risk-taker. It kept me going back.

These insights helped me focus on my life so I could develop healthier relationships and a more balanced lifestyle. Now the risks I take are those that come from being honest with myself and others. The excitement I get comes from creative expression and being accepted as myself.

95. PLEASE LISTEN TO WHAT I'M NOT SAYING

Don't be fooled by me. Don't be fooled by the face I wear. For I wear a mask; I wear a thousand masks I am afraid to take off, and none of them are me.

I give you the impression that I'm secure, that confidence is my name and coolness my game, that the water's calm and I'm in command, and that I need no one. But don't believe me. Please.

My surface may seem smooth—underneath I dwell in confusion, in fear, in aloneness. But I hide this. I panic at the thought of my weakness and fear being found out. That's why I frantically create a mood to hide behind, a calm, sophisticated front to shield me from the glance that knows. But such a glance is my salvation and I know it. It's the only thing that can assure me of acceptance and love. I'm afraid you'll think less of me, that you'll laugh. Laughter would kill me.

So I play my game, my desperate pretending game, with a front of "having it together," and a trembling child within. And so my life becomes a front. I chatter to you in a cool tone; I tell you everything that's nothing and nothing of what's everything, of what's crying within me. So when I go into my routine do not be fooled by what I am saying. Please listen to what I'm not saying.

I dislike the phony game I'm playing. I'd like to be real and spontaneous, and me. You've got to hold out your hand even when it may seem to be the last thing I want, or need. Only you can call me into aliveness. Each time you're kind and gentle, and encouraging, each time you try to understand because you really care, my heart begins to grow wings—small wings, very feeble wings.

I want you to know how important you are to me, how you can be a creator of the person that is me if you choose to. But it will not be easy for you. A long time of feeling inferior builds strong walls.

The nearer you approach me, the harder I may strike back. It is irrational, but I **am** irrational. I fight against the very things I cry out for. But I am told that love is stronger than walls, and therein lies my hope. Please try to beat down those walls with firm hands, but with gentle hands—for a child is very sensitive.

Who am I, you may wonder? I am someone you know very well. I am every newcomer you meet.

96. PARENT BASHING (THE CLOCK)

As a newcomer, I had a great deal of difficulty understanding how people could be nice to their parents. After all the hurt and humiliation, the neglect, abuse, and abandonment, how could we not be angry? I listened in meetings as people shared about recognizing the anguish of growing up. I heard and felt the pain as they told about their childhoods. These experiences, combined with my own Step work, seemed to fuel my anger.

I could hardly breathe as I recognized the pain and confusion brought on by my family's system of communication and recognition. My anger choked me physically and mentally. I became obsessed with ideas of lashing out at them and getting even. How could any decent human, or even one not so decent, treat their own as I was treated? How could they have been so blind?

I learned that a key word in recovery is "process." It can be likened to a clock. At 3 o'clock, or 6, or 9, you can use the clock, but all the hours together are needed for the whole clock. Our goal is 12, but until the process reaches that number, we have to be exactly where we are, no matter what. We can't let ourselves get stuck there, or like the clock, we lose time. A clock is not useful if it runs fast or slow or quits. We share our gratitude for meetings, our sponsors, and our friends in the Program.

Finding the difference between accountability and blaming comes through sharing feelings on a regular basis with others in recovery. This is how we keep our clocks ticking. We need to feel all the feelings. Others also feared they would be stuck in parent-bashing. One member called it a refuge for the emotionally irresponsible. By keeping in the process, we're able to use our feelings of anger and abandonment as a tool for identifying our authentic selves.

By the time I had finished Step Eight, I had learned a new attitude and had had a change of heart. In Step Nine, I was set free. I came to realize that my parents had done what they had done, but I had developed new boundaries and a new way of life which allowed me to live in the spirit of love and forgiveness. I no longer felt a need to punish, change, chastise, or harass my parents. I gave back to them the responsibility of their actions, by owning my own. I knew that what they did with it was no longer any of my business.

I can laugh about the clock, but it was my biggest tool to stay in today. It ticks with my heart. Today, my parents are not my punching bag, and I am not theirs. The solution is the spiritual process we call recovery. It must have all the numbers to be complete.

97. SERVICE

Being of service in recovery was the beginning of my life. It was the first place I could safely practice my new boundary-setting skills. It helped me to feel part of the group in a tangible way. It gave me a sense of self-worth I had not known before.

I joined a home group and became part of a new "family." My family members welcomed me. By taking a job (making coffee), I felt I was useful. I became *very* useful. I added setting up to my job list, and took it upon myself to make sure the restrooms were clean. Within three months, I found I barely had time to pay attention in meetings.

Our chairperson called a home group business meeting. To my surprise, they complimented me on my hard work and enthusiasm. Then they fired me! I was astonished.

At coffee after the meeting, each person shared their experiences in service. They all said the same thing: we spent our lives too busy to love ourselves, take care of ourselves, nurture ourselves, pay attention to ourselves, or heal ourselves. Our meetings and our recovery must be focused on our own healing. Service work is one tool, but like any tool, it can be misused by codependents.

My new family loved me enough to set some boundaries and teach me how to set some for myself. I've been in recovery over a year now, and have another service position. This time it's different. My service work is part of my self-nurturing and healing. I have the freedom to say no, not just yes, yes, yes.

98. WHAT I'VE LEARNED

I've learned how to channel anger in the right direction and not take it out on myself or on others. When I get on my little "Pity Pot" I have to stop and think is this worth relapsing over? No! Be thankful for what my Higher Power has given me.

I no longer need to lie and put on any phony fronts. People now accept me for what I am but, most important, I accept myself.

Everything does not have to go my way or be what I want it to be. My way wasn't too hot to begin with. This way of life is much better.

I have many more choices now when I am troubled. There are meetings, my sponsor, fellow members, and most of all my Higher Power. I don't have to suffer the mental pain alone. When I share it with someone else, the burden is lightened. Keeping busy has given me a good many days in recovery. Early on in the Program I was told to get involved. Well, I did as I was told and I cannot really tell you all the many benefits that I have been given. My time spent in service has helped me so much.

I won't slide back into codependency if I work the Program. I will not regain all the misery and guilty feelings I had for many years.

Recovery has given me what nothing else has been able to: the will to go on with life, the tools which are the 12 Steps to deal with life on a daily basis.

The Program has saved my life. On many days before, I did not think it was worth saving. Recovery comes first because without it, I have nothing.

99. MAKING GOOD CHOICES

I never wanted to say yes or no to anything. I was always stuck. I felt paralyzed when I had to make a decision, even one as simple as which meal to order at a restaurant. When I had a big choice to make, such as buying a new car, I would go around and around, talking constantly about alternatives and asking everyone what I should do. I drove my friends and family crazy with my "wishy-washy" attitude.

In recovery, I discovered some of the reasons why decisions were so hard for me. I was afraid to make a mistake. My parents were very rigid and always concerned with "what the neighbors would think." They seldom showed me any affection. When I did something they considered wrong, they jumped all over me. As an adult, I was still trying to figure out what was "right."

I have gradually learned to rely on and respect my own choices. Every day, I acknowledge all the little decisions I have made, and give myself credit for them. I still make mistakes, but now I accept them as part of being human. I am becoming comfortable with making decisions.

100. WISHES FOR THE NEWCOMER

May you find serenity and peace in a world you may not always understand. May the pain you have known and the conflict you have experienced give you the strength and courage to stay in recovery, facing each new situation with courage and hope. Always know that there are those whose love and understanding will always be there, even when you feel most alone. May you discover enough goodness in others to believe in the goodness in you. May a kind word, a reassuring touch, and a warm smile be yours every day, and may you give these gifts as well as receive them. Remember the sunshine when the storm seems unending. Teach love to those who know hate, and let that love help you make spiritual progress.

May the teachings of your sponsor become part of you, so that you may call upon them and pass them on. Remember, those whose lives you have touched and who have touched yours are always a part of you, even if the encounters were less than you would have wished. May you not become too worried with material things, but instead place value on the goodness in your heart. Find time in each day to see beauty and love in the world around you. Realize that each person has abilities, but each of us is different in our own way.

What you may feel you lack in one area may be more than compensated for in another. What you feel you lack in the present may become one of your strengths in the future. May you see your future as one filled with promise and possibility. Learn to view everything as a worthwhile experience. May you find enough inner strength to determine your own worth by yourself, and not be dependent on another's judgment of your accomplishments. May you always feel welcome and loved.

101. GET TO THE POINT

When I first was able to share at meetings, I would say my name and then didn't know what else to say. I knew I wanted to share my heart, the pain I had been through, and the freedom I found at the end of each meeting, but the words wouldn't come.

I kept coming back, though. At coffee after the meetings (a regular activity of my home group), I was able to share a little more. Some of the other new people expressed anger at not having enough time to talk. My home group uses a timer. The speaker has five to seven minutes, then the buzzer goes off. Individuals have three to four minutes. Each person gets a warning to "wrap it up" as their time runs out. I didn't feel angry; I just felt frustrated.

Finally I was able to bring up the subject of the timer, and ask the older members to share about it and about the frustration I felt as a newcomer. Many of them smiled as I looked around the room. Gently, but with humor, I discovered that the point of the timer was to get to the point.

The older members explained that one common characteristic of codependency was a lack of trust. This aspect of the disease created time problems in meetings. Many people took sharing time to find their comfort zone and feel safe. Once they reached their own safety level, after sharing about trivial matters, they could talk about what they really needed to say. The group supported each person finding safety and trust in meetings, but the need for members to share had created a dilemma. Many members talked on and on, trying to locate a "trust zone." If someone got up for coffee, or left the room, some members' "trust levels" were affected and they felt abandoned, rejected, or ignored.

Recovery means learning to trust, but it also means learning boundaries and finding trust within ourselves. The home group instituted the buzzer system to facilitate room for more people to share. Home group "jobs" were established to allow members to feel part of the group externally. Each job has two co-workers. This provides an opportunity for many members to be involved. The jobs are rotated monthly, including the job of timer.

The timer works as a tool to help each member learn to think before speaking. Because we often are not in touch with our own reality, this process offers us an opportunity to clarify our thoughts before sharing.

After hearing all this, I felt less frustrated; in fact, I felt hopeful. I learned my feelings were normal, and that many others had experienced them. I learned that one more time, recovery in all its aspects requires a process.

102. COMPUTERS INSTEAD OF PEOPLE

I became a computer programmer because that job let me interact with machines instead of people. I had no confidence in my ability to relate to other human beings. I did my best to make myself invisible.

I started going to CoDA meetings because I wanted to feel better about myself. With the help of my sponsor and the other members, I am beginning to understand why I had so much trouble placing value on what I thought, felt, or said.

I was the middle child in a family where most of the attention focused on my father's alcoholism. My little brother was always in trouble, and my older sister always played the hero, rescuing him. I was mostly ignored, and in fact learned to become so inconspicuous that I nearly disappeared. I spent a lot of my time at the video arcade, playing games. Computer programming was another way to escape from the pain of reality.

Thanks to CoDA, I've learned that my quietness and listening abilities have a positive side, too. They seem to encourage other people to express themselves. I've become a liaison at work between the programmers and the tech writers, and have been able to resolve several problems that were causing trouble between the two groups. I am learning to get in touch with my own feelings and am trying hard to express myself more. I no longer feel that computers are more fun than people.

103. PRAYER AND MEDITATION

We're told that trying to pray *is* praying. "Oh, God, help me! If you get me out of this mess, I'll never screw up again." This was our favorite prayer before we entered the Program. We were always bargaining with God.

We have learned new prayers and a new way to talk and listen to our Higher Power. We are seeking God's will for us. Many of us had to learn *how* to pray. We began with very simple prayers: "God, help me know Your will for me." "Thank you, God, for helping me today."

We learn that prayer helps us with our overdependence on people, places, and things by giving us the insight and strength to rearrange our priorities. Prayer doesn't change God, but it changes those who pray.

Today in our prayers, we seek our Higher Power's will for us. We no longer bargain with God.

Prayer is seeking answers and direction in life. Meditation is listening for answers from a Higher Power and developing the faith within us to accept those answers. Reflection is finding ways to change the answers we get from prayer and meditation into *action*.

Reflection is understanding how to use the Twelve Steps. It is not snap judgment. It asks us to think of the pros and cons of our possible choices and to understand what directions we will take to give us the best results.

The progress of spirituality from prayer to meditation to reflection is active, not passive. It is taking part in the joy of putting the results of prayer and meditation into action.

We have learned through times of quiet reflection to work into our lives the answers our Higher Power has given us as a result of our prayer and meditation.

104. ARE YOU READY FOR A NEW RELATIONSHIP?

When this topic came up at a meeting, I was astounded. I had heard that the rule was, "no new relationships in the first year," that the only relationship I needed to work on was the one between me and my Higher Power as expressed through my inner child. I had understood that all my love energies were to be directed toward loving, nurturing, and healing myself, that until I could love myself I certainly couldn't love another.

At this meeting, I heard differently. Several members said that they found the only way they could find personal validation was through a romantic relationship. It was only in this context that they felt they deserved to receive the recognition to meet their needs. Yes, some said they had grown out of early relationships; some said their relationships were currently rocky at best; and some said their partners had joined them in recovery. They all said that being in a relationship had forced them to look at themselves. They'd learned they could no longer blame the other person. This resulted in being forced into establishing boundaries and sticking up for themselves.

Pain was a common word in each of their stories. Whether or not having a relationship was a necessary journey, they didn't know. Some regretted it, but all agreed that they believed their Higher Powers had been there daily.

One woman said, "Give me a room full of men, and I will choose the only sociopath." It drew a laugh, but also a sigh. She said she believed we were attracted to people who were like us in emotional, spiritual, and mental recovery.

As the meeting came to a close, I knew the answer to my question, "Am I ready for a relationship?" could only be answered by me, with the help of my Higher Power.

105. STEP EIGHT

With the clarity provided when we take Steps Four and Five, and the responsibility for our actions we learn from living Steps Six and Seven, we are prepared for Steps Eight and Nine. The preparation the Steps lead us through is essential if we are to continue to recover from codependency. Acceptance of our own past and present, and integration of this knowledge into our daily lives is evident as we approach Steps Eight and Nine. If we have not yet learned to practice this honesty, willingness, open-mindedness, responsibility, and humility, we must return to the previous Steps.

Step Eight requires a list of all we have harmed. Using our Fourth Step list as a guide, we review it and add anyone we had forgotten. We make sure our own name is on the list, for in harming others we have also harmed ourselves and allowed ourselves to be harmed.

Once our list is finished, we are invited to become willing to make amends. Understanding this part of the Step is essential to the spiritual journey to which we have committed ourselves. The dictionary defines "amends" as *something given or done to make up for loss or injury that one has caused.* "Amend" (singular) is defined as *to make better, improve, correct, or to improve one's conduct.* These definitions, combined with the knowledge of our spiritual quest through the Steps, include action and change. Our action is the willingness to carry out the Ninth Step. This comes from a change of attitude.

"To become willing" is the process we use to change our attitude. We have learned, through the previous Steps, a new outlook on life. From "half-empty" we have changed to seeing life as "half-full." Our change in thinking is literally an effort on our part to change our thoughts. We may be tempted to fall back into old ways of thinking, but we forge ahead, courageously asking our Higher Power's strength to guide us. We also remind ourselves repeatedly of the Steps we have taken and the strength each one has given us in our resolve to change.

If any doubt lingers as to our responsibility to those we have harmed, we review the list with our sponsors.

106. STEP NINE

As we pray for guidance in becoming willing to make amends to all we have harmed, we begin to experience a change of heart. We begin to see our faults more clearly. We know where we were wrong. In spite of the fact that for years we have seen more clearly how the other person harmed us, we dismiss these thoughts. We know now that the other person is none of our business. We know we are to walk in our own shoes only. We are grateful for this new attitude, and we experience a new sense of freedom from within.

Throughout our recovery, we've learned how to have a new style of relationship with others in recovery. Asking someone to sponsor us, becoming a member of a home group and taking part in the meetings, learning how to let other members share their stories without giving advice, learning to let others feel their feelings, and learning how to be a part of a new way of thinking and living have helped us set boundaries for ourselves. Step Nine gives us the opportunity to apply all we have learned in recovery. We've used the Steps to explore our old way of living codependently. Now we step out to demonstrate our changes in attitude, thinking, and actions. We open our lives for healing in relationships that may have been open wounds all our lives. We demonstrate our new boundaries by accepting responsibility for our wrongs. We begin to heal ourselves.

The healing process is part of our spiritual pathway. We heal, and we open the doors for others to heal. Our focus, however, remains on our wrongs, never on the wrongs of the person we approach with our amends. As specified in the Step, we make direct amends, in person when at all possible. We admit our fault in action and thought. We are cautioned by this Step to be aware of the impact of our amends on others. If we will hurt them, we find another way to make amends.

We demonstrate in our daily living, after our admission, how we have changed our behavior and thinking. "I'm sorry" isn't enough. We admit we were wrong and ask for forgiveness.

We cannot expect any results. Those are in God's hands. Our duty is simply to admit our faults.

If direct amends are not possible, we make amends in principle. We may do volunteer work, make anonymous donations, or write letters to those who have passed away. We are careful to discuss this process with our sponsors, to be certain we are not avoiding our responsibility.

Our Ninth Step sets up a new pattern for us to continue to stay real with people around us. We continue this effort on a daily basis.

107. HEALTHY HELPING

When "healthy helping" was chosen for a topic at my regular Thursday meeting I thought I was in an eating disorder meeting. That wasn't the case. The subject at hand was about recovering codependents learning how to distinguish between codependent helping and healthy helping.

I learned that, like me, many others had difficulty in making the transition from codependency into helping others. Fear of "making a mistake" and having the wrong motive for helping was common to all. Many also shared that they had gone from the over-helping of codependency to isolation out of fear of helping for the wrong reason.

This pattern of one extreme to the other was part of the process of recovery for many, but the balance that followed was also part of the process. This balance is healthy helping. It is a genuine response to need. The key, though, was that the response is to another's need, not our own.

In my codependent behavior, others' needs seemed to come first, but on examination, it was *my* need to avoid me and *my* need to manipulate others that motivated my actions. Codependent helping is grounded in fear, selfishness, shame, and denial. It is often doing for others what they can do for themselves, thus robbing them of their own self-respect and consequently causing them to resent me. Codependent helping is rescuing others. It crosses and violates others' boundaries. It perpetuates victim/victimizer roles. Codependent behavior demands that I ignore the child within me and my own feelings and focus on another person or situation. It does not allow me to honor either.

Healthy helping is joyous. It may involve self-sacrifice, but unlike codependent behavior, it does not involve denial of the self. We find the freedom to help others in a healthy way as we find the willingness to work and practice the Steps of recovery. The Steps help us see how to help ourselves in a nurturing and healthy way. They teach us to honor our own needs. In finding our own needs, and learning to ask that our needs be met, we learn to create boundaries.

Boundaries are the beginning of healthy helping. Although others' boundaries are invisible, we learn to recognize verbal clues of them. We learn to detach. Healthy helping comes from honoring and helping ourselves first. It seems contradictory, but once we have learned how to honor ourselves, we can then learn to honor others' selves. When we learn how to achieve this balance and maintain it, we have the freedom required for healthy helping. We can experience the joy of helping others for the right reasons.

Our heads have told us for years that we are helping for "good" reasons. Now we learn to listen to our guts. Our insides know. The child within, the inner voice, intuition, our higher mind, whatever we choose to call it, instinctively recognizes the difference between codependent and healthy helping. It takes practice, but it's worth it!

108. DON'T GIVE UP

If there's one thing I want to pass on to those who are struggling in recovery, it's "don't give up." Like me, a lot of people come into the Program after spending most of their lives "giving up," running away from situations that were too painful or required too much effort. It was easier to quit and find fault with things we didn't like.

It's easy to give up on a problem too quickly. A long effort at finding a solution is sometimes painful and irritating. But we learn by working the 12 Steps that the answers do come if we continue to do the research—through study and prayer, one day at a time.

Courage is what makes us do the right thing even when we want to give up. We can find happiness while surrounded by darkness; we can be kind in the middle of hate and jealousy; we can have peace of mind when we're surrounded by confusion, fear, and anger. What has helped me is knowing and remembering that there isn't much I can't handle today that my Higher Power, fellow members, and myself can't handle together.

I'm not a quitter or a loser any more.

109. LETTING GO

To let go doesn't mean to stop caring; it means I can't do it for someone else.

To let go is not to cut myself off; it is the realization that I can't control another.

To let go is not to enable, but to allow learning from natural consequences.

To let go is to admit powerlessness, which means the outcome is not in my hands.

To let go is not to try to change or blame another; I can only change myself.

To let go is not to care for, but to care about.

To let go is not to fix, but to be supportive.

To let go is not to judge, but to allow another to be a human being.

To let go is not to be in the middle arranging outcomes, but to allow others to effect their own outcomes.

To let go is not to be protective; it is to permit another to face reality.

To let go is not to deny, but to accept.

To let go is not to nag, scold, or argue, but to search out my own shortcomings and to correct them.

To let go is not to adjust everything to my desires, but to take each day as it comes and to cherish the moment.

To let go is not to criticize and regulate anyone, but to try to become what I dream I can be.

To let go is not to regret the past, but to grow and live for the future.

To let go is to fear less and love more.

110. FAMILY HERO

I scheduled a special appointment with my family doctor. I wanted to know why I was always tired, why I always had a headache, and why I seemed to catch every bug that came around. I was shocked when Dr. Ross suggested that my hectic lifestyle and problems communicating with my parents could be affecting my health.

A friend recommended I read a book about adult children of dysfunctional families. I was surprised to discover I had all the characteristics of the family hero, one of the typical roles children from such families assume. I had been captain of the girls' volleyball team, a straight A student, and editor of the school newspaper. Now I was the hero of my sales team because of my successful sales record.

As I looked back over my life, I realized I had been trying to convince my parents I could meet their expectations, even though they'd made it clear to me that they had really wanted a boy. Meeting their expectations meant that I neglected my own needs.

As a result of entering recovery, I was able to slowly let go the need for my parents' approval. I found a new place to live—on the other side of town from my parents' home. I began to look at other careers.

It's taken over a year to get in touch with how I feel about my childhood. I'm working on forgiving my parents for their unrealistic expectations of me. I'm a lot healthier and happier now.

111. SHAME

In understanding shame, I learned to compare it to driving my car. Shame is the regulator that identifies when I am going too fast or too slow. When I exceed the limits of my humanity, I feel shame. This healthy feeling reminds me of my humanity, that I have limits, and allows me to acknowledge my need for a Higher Power.

When I drive, I am not a single unit of car and driver. The car has limits. Shame is my clutch in life. When I drive too slow in a gear, my car lugs along, and when I don't live up to my own principles, I get a lugging feeling of shame. When I drive too fast in a gear, my car pulls and whines, and doesn't drive smoothly. Shame reminds me that I'm not the whole enchilada in life. I am the human and God is the God. Shame is not a good/bad issue. It is a reminder of my natural limits as a human. Like a clutch, I use it to shift gears.

As a codependent living in the disease, I didn't experience healthy shame. I confused shame and guilt, good and bad. I felt *bad*, unworthy, less than. My sense of self was connected to my clutch, so whenever I felt less than perfect (or felt human), I felt *bad*. I shifted into a growing and continual downward spiral of shame.

This is almost universal for codependents. From unrealistic expectations of our abilities and capabilities in childhood, we learned to feel unhealthy shame. We were not who our parents wanted us to be. The truth was we never could or would be. It wasn't *humanly* possible. When we couldn't catch the ball, or didn't dress the way they wanted, when we couldn't fix their emotions, we felt unhealthy shame. We thought we were responsible. We accepted the shame that belonged to others because of their own actions, opinions, and expectations. We internalized shame, and each time we felt it again, we unloaded our whole truck full.

Getting rid of unhealthy shame is accomplished through working the Steps and learning to nurture ourselves. As we grow in recovery, we are able to give back the unhealthy shame. We learn to have healthy shame.

Shame becomes a welcome tool, instead of a plague reminding us of our unhealthy lives. We were never God, and were not meant to fix everything. Instead of feeling unhealthy shame for this, we now can celebrate that we *know* we aren't God, and are grateful that we're not.

112. CHANGE IS A PROCESS

Over an indefinite period of time, we are all asked to make a lot of changes in our lives when we begin our recovery. Those changes will take time. They're an ongoing process which won't happen overnight. We won't see a bolt of lightning come down and strike us, changing us, making us all better.

None of us have it all together, and there's nothing wrong with admitting that. Sometimes we may need to take time out to work on ourselves. We may not have much to say at a meeting. Every positive change we make in our recovery makes us a better person. Some of us may ask what it is exactly that we need to change. I was told that I needed to change "everything I say, everything I think, and everything I do." That was overwhelming, but I knew it was true. I began to realize and accept that change meant growth.

Change in recovery isn't so difficult. It's our resistance to it that makes it difficult. "Change is a process, not an event."

113. SPIRITUAL RATHER THAN RELIGIOUS

People in recovery through Twelve Step programs hear phrases such as "the spiritual part of the program" or "this is a spiritual program." Twelve Step programs clearly separate themselves from religions, and yet are equally clear in claiming to be spiritual programs. What does it mean to be "spiritual rather than religious"?

One simple way of understanding spirituality is to see that it is concerned with our ability, through our attitudes and actions, to relate to others, to ourselves, and to God as we understand Him. All of us have a way of relating to our own lives, other people, and

God which tends either to be positive, healthy, fulfilling, and life-giving, or tends toward the negative, self-
defeating, and destructive. The question is not
whether we will be spiritual, but whether we are moving in the direction of a negative or positive spirituality.

Spirituality is a simple way of living. It seems
there are four basic movements that recovering people
need to make to put their lives on a positive spiritual
basis. The first of these is a movement from fear to
trust; the second, from self-pity to gratitude; the third,
from resentment to accepance; and the fourth, from
dishonesty to honesty.

114. GUILT

As long as we could be the guilty one, we had
some sense of control in our surroundings. This got
pretty far out for us sometimes. When a partner had a
bad day, we claimed the guilt. Had we just been nicer
at breakfast, or dinner the night before, or Christmas
ten years ago, this wouldn't have happened. Even at
times when we knew it wasn't our fault, we still got
the feelings anyway.

We often felt we were guilty by nature. "If it
weren't for me, the world would be a better place.
Everyone would be happier."

We learn by working the Steps to recognize and accept only the guilt that is our own. Guilt becomes the feeling we get when we violate our own value systems. It is a healing tool once we learn to own only what is ours.

In the past, we frequently confused it with shame or embarrassment. We begin to tell the difference once we've taken our own inventory and learned to practice and continually identify our feelings with Step Ten. We can ask ourselves, "Did I go against my own value system here? How?" Sometimes we may also feel shame, but we learn to separate the two feelings.

Guilt allows us to practice the principle of responsibility. It gives us authority over our own actions. It protects our own boundaries, and lets us respect others' boundaries. If we accept guilt which is not ours, we cheat others out of a tool that they, too, need in order to lead a healthy life.

When I feel guilty, I look for where I am wrong and admit it. I check with my sponsor to identify the correct behavior and follow through. Guilt no longer sucks me into playing God or seeking control. Of myself, I am powerless, but with God and the values He has helped me identify, I have freedom.

115. HEALING

I was married for twenty years to my first wife, who suffered from serious depression. She was hysterical almost daily, and abused me verbally when I finally gave up trying to talk to her.

My second marriage nearly ended in divorce, too, before I got into recovery. I felt overwhelmingly anxious every time my wife got moody. I would try to "fix" her moods, and make her happy. I saw any deviation from "normal" as a possible recurrence of what I had gone through before. I was nervous, depressed, and suspicious of every little change in my wife's attitude. I spent money we really couldn't afford to spend, buying her gifts to assure her I loved her. I kept my own "bad times" bottled up inside me, in order that she not be worried. Our relationship was claustrophobic, instead of having the intimacy I craved.

With the help of my group and my Higher Power, I'm learning to sort out what belongs to this marriage and what is still unhealed from my first one. CoDA has really helped me understand why I react the way I do. I'm learning to care *about* my wife, not care *for* her.

116. MEDITATION

"Twenty-One Ways to Get Out of Your Body" was the name of a tape a friend gave me to learn meditation. It seemed ridiculous at the time, but through Step meetings, I learned that meditation is a tool we use to get out of our own way in order to listen to God. People had differing ways to do this. I learned that each explored the various ways available through other members and literature before adopting what fit them best.

The meditative state I have learned to use I call "practicing the presence of God." I began to learn this practice by reading a set of daily meditation books. I sat at my kitchen table and focused on my reading. I focused on the color of the sky, the smell of the air, the feel of the wind. My favorite was:

"In the quiet of this morning hour, I come to Thee for peace and power to view the world through love-filled eyes, be gentle, understanding, wise. To see Thy children as Thou seest them ...."

I don't remember all of it, but it set a tone for me to practice the principles of love, forgiveness, humility, honor, and gratitude all day.

As I grew in recovery, I learned to establish a meditative state by listening to music and breathing. I took twenty breaths in and twenty out, breathing *in*

God's love and breathing *out* each specific dilemma I faced. These ranged daily from "What will I do about xxx?" or "What if xxx does or doesn't happen?" to specific personalities that I wanted to change or control even though I knew it was none of my business. I breathed out these people's names and released them to my God, and I breathed in God's love and wisdom. Listening to music, I drifted off in peace. It isn't really sleep, but just a sense of calmness and gratitude combined with a sense of knowing that I am honestly seeking to experience and pay attention to the voice within me where my God speaks to me.

Whenever I do this, I feel different afterwards. It doesn't always come easily, but now I look forward to it, and find it as refreshing and as supportive as my home group. It has become a necessary part of my day.

I have established an invitation place where I keep my meditation books and music. Because my concept of a Higher Power includes plants and animals, I have animal statues, and some sage and cedar at my invitation place. I have a picture of my spiritual leader, and a candle there. These are what I use. This is my place to invite my Higher Power to remind me He is God, I am not. I am a co-creator as I live in principle. As I ask questions in prayer to my God, my answers come, sometimes right away in meditation, but most often later in the day or week. It feels like something clicks, and I know that this is the highest best, and that my God has answered my prayers.

Practicing this conscious contact is the mainstay of my recovery. Without it I could not support the spiritual journey.

117. STEP TEN

Step Ten is my tool to pay attention. The direction in this Step requires that I check my awareness level of myself, instead of focusing on others. In the first nine Steps, I learned a new sense of peace and freedom I had never before experienced. It was an empowering feeling. Using the Tenth Step, I give myself a way to refocus if I need to, to find my power again. This Step also gives me a way to pat myself on the back. Step Ten is not like my old way of controlling myself so that I seemed to be living an acceptable life. Step Ten is about honestly appraising and honoring myself. It gives me a chance to stop and see whether I'm on track.

Step Ten keeps me human. It allows me to be imperfect. I have the freedom to be wrong. Instead of the old way of punishing myself with guilt, I have a way to own my mistakes and admit my wrongs. This process honors me. It gives me a way to be responsible for my behavior. It keeps me in balance.

118. STEP ELEVEN

Step Eleven gives me the tools to honor my voice within, to listen to it, and to take the appropriate actions necessary. It tells me to stay in touch and improve the contact I have established with my Higher Power.

My prayers are sometimes formal, sometimes spontaneous. They are the external expression of my desire to have my God direct my thinking and my actions. I pray every morning and every night, but I also pray all day. I imagine the word "God" in the center of my head to stop my brain from worry and fear, and I listen to what my heart tells me to do.

My days are not always the way I think they should be, but with Step Eleven, I have the freedom to trust the direction of my God. By thinking about God, I don't have to think about fear. I can choose to turn my thoughts to a realistic inventory of a situation and not get caught in the what-abouts or what-ifs.

My meditation began with reading a daily meditation book. In the morning, I used the book to give me a positive focus for the day. This process has expanded to include a daily *quiet time* where I focus on relaxing and breathing. With each breath, I breathe out my worries and breathe in my God's love and harmony. This process helps me bypass my busy mind and listen to my inner voice. It helps me throughout the day to stay in conscious contact with God, for with each breath, I renew my connection.

119. STEP TWELVE

My spiritual awakening was not a sudden flash of insight. It was a growing inner strength resulting from disciplined practice of the Steps. It was disciplined in that I did it even when I didn't want to. I did it when my feelings said I wasn't worth it, or that I was bad. I trusted the process, even when it seemed to be failing me. Like a jogger who slowly builds up to the marathon, I too built up to awakening. It was slow, painful, and seemed meaningless at times, but I kept on. My awakening came when I discovered I now had the tools to keep living in a world that had always seemed to reject me. I discovered that no matter what the world said, I had a way to honor me, and it was me who needed to honor me.

At times when I have quit jogging (so to speak), it takes me less than a day to lose the spiritual connection I've found in the Steps. I believe that maintenance is a daily effort (and I mean *effort*) until it becomes a daily gift. The Steps are almost automatic now. I have a freedom and peace that I never knew was possible. As long as I nurture it, it is mine. When I don't nurture it, I lose it at once.

Step Twelve confirms what the other Steps have taught me. My life is a spiritual journey, not a perfect jumping-off place where I can rest. Step Twelve is a way for me to do the kind of helping I always dreamed of, honoring myself and others. I cannot practice Step Twelve without the other Steps. It is the others that give me the appropriate boundaries so that I can give to other people.

My giving is as much a way of life as it is a specific action for any individual. It is standing up when I need to, and being quiet as well. It is joyous. It provides for laughter and love. It gives me room to be me. It gives me the freedom to move on, to grow, and to live. It gives me freedom to have intimacy, to love and be loved. My life is work; it is freedom; it is joy; it is sometimes painful. I am grateful.

120. PUSHING BUTTONS

Our family, parents, and loved ones can "push our buttons," and some say that's because they installed them.

Many of us grew up filled with shame, and it has continued into our later lives. Codependency and shame go together. We were told we could do better in school. We were told we weren't living up to our potential. We learned there was *something* wrong with us. We *should* do better. Guilt is when we make a mistake; shame is when we believe we *are* a mistake.

Our recovery allows us to identify and work out of our shame-filled past. We can't force the people in our lives who push our buttons to change. We *can* change our attitudes and the way we react to button-pushers and the old unmanageable tapes in our heads. Not being perfect no longer means not being worthwhile.

Today, we're learning not to let the button-pushers affect our outlook. Our sponsor and friends are always there to make sure our button-pushers have much less power over us.

121. FEAR OF EMPOWERMENT

Working the Steps, taking turns with jobs at my home group, attending meetings, and talking to my sponsor and other recovering codependents, kept me in a whirlwind of activity. There was always one more Step to work, more practice, and more trial and error. It was hard and painful, but I was learning a new way to live. I think my preoccupation with recovery bordered on obsession at times. This stage of recovery was necessary for me. After working Step Four, I found I wanted to slow down. As instructed, I did Step Five, but Six and Seven seemed less urgent.

As always, pain surfaced in my life and urged me slowly on through the Steps. By Eight and Nine, I found I didn't want to go to any more Step meetings, or call my sponsor. I shared about these feelings in a meeting where I knew my sponsor wouldn't be in attendance. I found out that many others shared my fears.

Once I had found this new way of life, owned it, and it was mine for the taking, I had a hard time taking it. The old feelings of "less than" and "what's the use" came up. I had been practicing not doing my codependent dances, and now was the time to start doing and getting in the habit of doing recovery dances.

The women who shared their experience, strength, and hope with me said they had learned society did not always reward women who said no to codependency. Somehow, self-negation in women had become popular and expected. Getting past the fear of rejection from work places, family, and a soci-

ety which had become used to victimizing its weak
(and many times its women) would demand that I live
close to my Higher Power.

This new way of life meant asking to have my
needs met, nurturing myself, and taking care, not
caretaking. It meant that what family, job, or society
thought was *not my business*. This was very hard for
me.

It really took and continues to take practice for me
to affirm myself and stand firm with my values. I
have learned it is not always a popular place to be. I
have also learned that my fear of empowerment has
been based on my fear that my God forgot to make
room for me in life. For so long, I failed to take my
rightful place at the banquet of life. I thought I didn't
belong. Now being at the banquet sometimes makes
me feel I am an unwanted guest. This is in my head.
There are no guests. We are all invited. I am wrong
when I don't take my rightful place.

The awkwardness of being at the banquet is
slowly wearing off with practice. I am now able to
use Steps Ten, Eleven, and Twelve to help me stay at
the table. Sharing these feelings with others helps me
know and remember that I am not alone. This helps
tremendously. In spite of my feelings, I have a re-
newed commitment to work the maintenance Steps.

When I do, my fear of empowerment lessens and I gratefully accept the reality of being at the banquet. As I practice, I become much more comfortable in this new way of living.

122. ATTITUDE OF GRATITUDE

When I first came into this Program and heard "have an attitude of gratitude" at a meeting, it made me sick to my stomach. I had nothing, at that time, to be grateful for. The last thing I wanted to hear was that mushy crap about gratitude and how good everyone felt and how grateful they were.

At the time I was full of anger, fear, resentment, guilt, and confusion. I had no idea what gratitude was or how to get it. I kept on going to the meetings, kept on listening, and kept on keeping my mouth shut. I eventually started to see what these people were talking about.

I had been dwelling only on the negative, rather than finding the positive. I was only looking at what I *didn't* have, rather than being grateful for what I *did* have. In order for me to be grateful, there were a few things I needed to do, and I found myself doing them on a daily basis. First I had to simply stop what I was doing and think. I share with my Higher Power and turn over my ungrateful feelings. I take a look at my past (go back over my First Step), then look at where I am now and where I'm heading—without future tripping, of course. Then I think about how much better I feel, both physically and mentally. I accept that I need to forgive myself and become more humble, and that I must live in the present.

Then I can become grateful. I can be grateful to my Higher Power for watching over me and guiding me. I can be grateful for my recovery—my new life. I can be grateful for the support of my family and friends. I can be grateful for what I have, rather than what I don't have. I can be grateful and accept my codependency for making me the person I am today, rather than blaming it.

Today, I *am* grateful.

123. FORGIVENESS

After twenty years of marriage, my husband wanted a divorce to marry someone else.

I was hurt and afraid. I loved him. I felt that losing him was a death of a large part of myself. No matter how I tried to explain to him that he was just in a mid-life crisis, he was determined. I then tried to "help" him adjust to our divorce by recommending different counselors and support groups. These tactics all failed, and left me feeling ashamed and terrible about myself. I decided to take my own advice, and began attending meetings of a codependency group.

I believe now that some of what I need to do to forgive my ex-husband involves understanding myself better. Forgiving him means letting go of him. In recovery, I've come to see how mistaken I was to think I could hold on to him by hanging on to my anger. It was as if there would be an empty space in my heart if I stopped reacting to him and his behavior. I couldn't seem to imagine ever filling that space with positive thoughts. Now I see that this "logic" didn't make much sense. I understand how I used resentment as a connection to him, hurting myself much more than him. I need a new life of my own, completely separate from his. Thanks to CoDA, I'm working on it.

124. ON THE BUS OR NOT?

Learning to leave behind me people and relationships that were not part of my recovery has been difficult. Many of the people in my life before recovery knew me more as a doormat or a sponge than as a person. Being a person in recovery has forced me (as long as I want to stay in recovery) to live this new way. It is no longer O.K. to abuse me. My tolerance for abuse is going. It is no longer O.K. to ignore me. I deserve, need, and want recognition. It is no longer O.K. to criticize me, and tell me how I should or shouldn't live.

Making statements of my value to myself has helped me stop putting myself in abusive situations. I used to think it was O.K. that I suffered if others might find some success out of it, but that's no longer true for me.

I find that many of the people I allowed to mistreat me have disappeared, as though they were repelled by my new way of life. It is those few, especially family members, who have been the most difficult to let go.

I heard a speaker at a meeting describe it as "on the bus or not." She said that with the direction of the Serenity Prayer, she has learned everyone gets to choose. In recovery, we've chosen the bus. It is open to everyone. Just as we had to experience the necessary pain until we were ready to climb aboard, so do others.

I still see my family. I practice my principles when I'm with them. I am me. But I don't recruit or preach about recovery. I have learned that my actions speak the loudest. It is painful to be with them. I see the old family dynamics and how that old order is trying to re-establish itself when we meet together. I see the lashing out at me when I refuse to cooperate. I don't get sucked in. I have learned to limit the time I spend with family for my own health.

My major involvement in their lives is in my prayers. Letting go of the expectations that they will be different, and loving them for who they are, makes me realize they never have met my needs. I can love them anyway, and I get my needs met elsewhere. This makes our time together more fun. I no longer have to get angry with them for not being who I want them to be. My bus stops at their house, even though they are not yet on the bus. It also leaves their house when I need to go in order to take care of me. I believe we teach people how to treat us. After years of my teaching my family that it's O.K. to treat me badly, I know it will take a long time to teach them different. I am willing to invest that time. I am not willing to park my bus at their house. I pray for the day they might join me on the bus.

125. S.A.L.T.

As a recovering codependent, one of the acronyms that has helped me most is "S.A.L.T.": Stop Action, Listen, and Think. Now, when I get myself into a situation where I'm in conflict with someone else, instead of reacting to the conflict I do the following:

1.   **Stop Action**, so I can focus on how I am feeling. I take deep breaths, and try to get my bearings so I can detach from the other person's behavior.

2.   **Listen** to my "self-talk." Am I telling myself to change the other person, to get him or her to see my side? Do I feel afraid or threatened?

3.   **Think** about what I want to do. If I think about the choices I have, I can change my usual ways of reacting. This gives me a feeling of mastery over my actions, and the self-confidence to deal effectively with the conflict.

126. RISK AND THE CODEPENDENT

Risk is change. Risk-taking is hard for all people, but especially hard on codependents. Risk means facing fear. Facing fear is what most of us have spent a lifetime avoiding.

The main points that limit most of us in stepping out and opening ourselves to possibility are:

1.   It is difficult for us to talk about our feelings. Risk brings up *big* feelings, particularly fear, and we just can't talk about it and diffuse it.

2.   We expect to be perfect (and have been told repeatedly to be "strong, right, good" and "if you can't

do something right, don't do it at all"), and risk is about new actions or changes. We may not do it perfectly the first time or the second. We may not be "good" at it. It may not be "right" for us. It may require practice and work.

3.   Risk means being direct. We might have to talk face-to-face with someone we have "issues" with. We might have to approach directly a person to whom we are attracted. We may have to "own" our feelings. Instead of talking *about* a person, we may have to talk *with* them.

4.   There are other factors that affect us when we face risking. "Don't rock the boat" has been pounded into us, sometimes literally. "What will other people think?" may severely hinder our willingness to risk. At a fundamental level, we may not feel worthy or deserving of having change, growth, excitement, and reward in our lives.

Risk is basically about moving through the fear of stepping out of the mold and becoming different. Facing risk is a transforming experience. We are different people on the other side of risk.

So the question becomes "Where do I gain the courage to risk?" The motivation to risk comes from many sources. One of the major motivations is disgust. When we are thoroughly sick and tired of being or acting a certain way, we do something about it. All change is risky, as it involves the unknown. It may work or it may not. If we get disgusted enough, we'll try something new just in case it *might* work.

Fear is a huge motivator, as well as being a hindrance. If we're afraid we'll never change, or "it" will never change, we'll try anything, risk anything, for "it" to be different.

A less painful motivation for risking is developing willingness. Either through aspiration or inspiration we may be given an example or role model that shows us what is possible. Somebody who has moved through similar circumstances or the same kinds of pain and suffering and transcended it will inspire us. If they can do it, we can, too.

There is one more huge motivation for change— love. When we love, change and risk are the coin of the realm. When we are in pain, we will risk for ourselves. When we are in love, we will risk for others, as well as self.

We must become willing to risk if we are to change and become more whole and balanced. Love can be the goal as well as the method, in little or large ways. When we are willing to see others and ourselves as deserving of the best, and that changing and growth are *worth* the risk, we will choose to risk.

127. GRATITUDE

Many times during the attendance of meetings, I hear the words grateful and gratitude. I have no doubt that when people say these words they mean them. For me having gratitude or being grateful is not always easy. For one thing, problems you don't have, you don't consider. Another is the tendency to take things for granted. And another is the habit of looking at what you don't have (materially) rather than being *grateful* for what you do have.

In order for me to be truly grateful, there are a few things that I must do. The first is to *stop*. The second is to become reflective, look at my past, and see where I am today. The third is to stay in the present and try to get materialism out of the picture. The fourth is to think of all the problems I could have and don't. The fifth, think of how much better I feel physically and mentally. Sixth, realize that my recovery is only a gift based on my spiritual growth from my Higher Power on a daily basis. Seventh, realize that in order to be truly grateful, I must gain more humility. I must know that I have to become more patient, tolerant, understanding, and forgiving. Eighth, I must learn to turn it over, learn acceptance of myself and others, become more honest.

When I do all these things, *then* I can become grateful and have an attitude of gratitude.

128. RESENTMENT = POISON

Resentment is a deadly poison that seems to plague us all at times, even after some time of recovery, a problem that will no doubt plague us most of our lives. CoDA does try to help us become aware of its dangers.

CoDA has taught me that:

1. Resentment robs me of serenity.

2. Resentment makes happiness impossible.

3. Resentment uses up energy that could go into accomplishment.

4. Resentment can become an emotional habit, making us habitually feel that we are victims of injustice.

5. Resentment is an emotional rehashing of some event or circumstance of the past. You cannot win because you cannot change the past.

6. Resentment is not caused by other persons, circumstances, or events, but by our own emotional response.

One way to handle resentment is to decide how much resentment the person, circumstance, or event deserves (which is usually very little) or how much I need to suffer. With resentment, like anger, nobody suffers but me.

Then I have to say to myself, "Who needs it?" and call someone in CoDA and go to a meeting.

129. TRADITIONS AND RECOVERY

The Twelve Steps give us a pathway to follow so that as individuals we may establish healthy lives. The Traditions enable us to establish and maintain healthy groups.

Just as we have learned to recognize and value boundaries with one another, the Traditions guide our groups through the pitfalls of codependency on a larger basis.

Paralleling the Steps, the Traditions give us a focus and a set of principles to live by. We are reminded that our groups are not to be devoted to any one individual, that they should remain focused on what is common to all. Our authority is to be based on a loving Higher Power as expressed through a group conscience. This conscience is made up of the experience, strength, and hope of *all* members. It is achieved by discussion and sharing, not just a show of hands.

Tradition Three reminds us that to be a member we need only express our desire for healthy and loving relationships. It helps us remember that as long as we are working toward this goal, we can continue to be members.

Accepting and demonstrating responsibility on a group level is addressed in Tradition Four. Given the spiritual principles of our recovery, we have the autonomy and responsibility to take care of our own group. Tradition Five furthers this responsibility by reminding us that we carry the message of recovery to those codependents who still suffer.

In Tradition Six, we are cautioned about the dangers of losing sight of our purpose. In Seven, we are reminded to accept responsibility for our group, both financially and physically. Our support means we pay our own way, set up our own chairs, and learn to practice our personal boundaries in a group setting.

Tradition Eight gives us the freedom to stay a self-help organization, but acknowledges that we may employ paid professionals as Special Workers. In Tradition Nine, we are cautioned again against the rigidity that so colored our codependency. We do not organize (tell others what to do). It reminds us that job titles are job descriptions, not designations of power.

Recognizing our tendency to give our opinions, Tradition Ten reminds us of the spiritual nature of our journey and the need to understand the boundaries of the group. Other issues are not our business.

Tradition Eleven reinforces our individual and group boundaries by reminding us that what we do, not what we say, speaks of our recovery. No single person is a spokesman for CoDA. Tradition Twelve confirms this spiritual position by reminding us of anonymity. Without it, we are not able to place principles before personalities.

The Traditions allow us to live life, to survive codependency, to recover, and to share our recovery. They allow us, individually and collectively, to continue to grow in a healthy way. They give us freedom from the old ways of control and manipulation.

TWELVE STEPS OF
CO-DEPENDENTS ANONYMOUS

1. We admitted we were powerless over others—that our lives had become unmanageable.
2. Came to believe that a power greater than ourselves could restore us to sanity.
3. Made a decision to turn our will and our lives over to the care of God as we understood God.
4. Made a searching and fearless moral inventory of ourselves.
5. Admitted to God, to ourselves, and to another human being the exact nature of our wrongs.
6. Were entirely ready to have God remove all these defects of character.
7. Humbly asked God to remove our shortcomings.
8. Made a list of all persons we had harmed, and became willing to make amends to them all.
9. Made direct amends to such people wherever possible, except when to do so would injure them or others.
10. Continued to take personal inventory and when we were wrong, promptly admitted it.
11. Sought through prayer and meditation to improve our conscious contact with God as we understood God, praying only for knowledge of God's will for us and the power to carry that out.
12. Having had a spiritual awakening as the result of these steps, we tried to carry this message to other co-dependents, and to practice these principles in all our affairs.

The Twelve Steps reprinted for adaptation with permission of Alcoholics Anonymous World Services, Inc.

TWELVE TRADITIONS OF
CO-DEPENDENTS ANONYMOUS

1. Our common welfare should come first; personal recovery depends upon CoDA unity.

2. For our group purpose there is but one ultimate authority—a loving higher power as expressed to our group conscience. Our leaders are but trusted servants; they do not govern.

3. The only requirement for membership in CoDA is a desire for healthy and loving relationships.

4. Each group should remain autonomous except in matters affecting other groups or CoDA as a whole.

5. Each group has but one primary purpose—to carry its message to other co-dependents who still suffer.

6. A CoDA group ought never endorse, finance or lend the CoDA name to any related facility or outside enterprise, lest problems of money, property, and prestige divert us from our primary spiritual aim.

7. Every CoDA group ought to be fully self-supporting, declining outside contributions.

8. Co-Dependents Anonymous should remain forever nonprofessional, but our service centers may employ special workers.

9. CoDA, as such, ought never be organized; but we may create service boards or committees directly responsible to those they serve.

10. CoDA has no opinion on outside issues; hence the CoDA name ought never be drawn into public controversy.

11. Our public relations policy is based on attraction rather than promotion; we need always maintain personal anonymity at the level of press, radio, and films.

12. Anonymity is the spiritual foundation of all our Traditions, ever reminding us to place principles before personalities.

The Twelve Traditions reprinted for adaptation with permission of Alcoholics Anonymous World Services, Inc.

Inquiries, orders, and requests for
catalogs and special discount pricing
may be addressed to:

Glen Abbey Books, Inc.
P.O. Box 31329
Seattle, Washington 98103

Toll-free 24-hour
Order and Information Line
1-800-782-2239
(All U.S.)